encountering the unionized university

jack h. schuster
issue editor

Jossey-Bass Inc., Publishers
San Francisco • Washington • London

ENCOUNTERING THE UNIONIZED UNIVERSITY
New Directions for Higher Education
Volume II, Number 1, Spring 1974
Jack H. Schuster, Issue Editor

New Directions for Higher Education is published quarterly
by Jossey-Bass, Inc., Publishers. Subscriptions are available
at the regular rate for institutions, libraries, and agencies
of $25 for one year. Individuals may subscribe at the special
professional rate of $15 for one year. Single issues are
available only for orders of five or more copies at $3.75 each.
New Directions is numbered sequentially—please order extra copies
by sequential number. The volume and issue numbers above are
included for the convenience of libraries. Second-class postage
rates paid at San Francisco, California, and at additional mailing
offices.

Correspondence:
Subscriptions, single-issue orders, change of address notices,
undelivered copies, and other correspondence should be sent to
New Directions Subscriptions, Jossey-Bass, Inc., Publishers,
615 Montgomery Street, San Francisco, California 94111.
Editorial correspondence should be sent to the Editor-in-Chief,
JB Lon Hefferlin, at the same address.

Library of Congress Catalogue Card Number LC 74-2328

Cover design by Willi Baum
Manufactured in the United States of America

contents

editor's notes

Few developments in American higher education have caused as much consternation, anxiety, and frantic activity as the advent of faculty collective bargaining. Opinions within the academic community remain highly polarized. Some denounce faculty unionism as a blight leading inexorably to a wholesale transformation of academe, undermining the character of the American university, shattering the shared-authority model of governance, destroying the last vestiges of collegiality. Others, no less fervent, view faculty unionism as the sole means for defending the legitimate interests of beleaguered faculties and for preserving the essential values of the academic community against further encroachments by accountability-minded politicians, arbitrary administrators, cost-conscious trustees, and students bent on equal participation in academic policy-making.

This intensity of feeling is understandable, for collective bargaining agreements are a recent phenomenon in American education. And, so far, the process has not stabilized; the future configuration of collective bargaining, especially in four-year institutions of higher education, is unsettled, volatile, unpredictable. On one issue, though, many neutrals and partisans alike agree: faculty collective bargaining will be a formidable force in American higher education—possibly the most potent change agent to confront the academic community in the 1970s.

In this issue of *New Directions for Higher Education,* my colleagues and I explore, from quite different vantage points, faculty collective bargaining and its implications for higher education. We attempt in our reflections to move beyond the purely speculative nature of the early literature on the topic. Each of us probes different aspects of this complex phenomenon, basing our remarks wherever possible on first-hand involvement and observation.

My continuing research on the topic leads me to one dominant conclusion: the pluralism that characterizes American higher education generally is reflected anew in the widely differing characteristics of faculty unionism from one setting to the next. In spite of this complexity, however, certain trends are emerging, and we examine them in these pages.

To lead off the issue, Henry Mason, an authority on campus

governance, explores the many links between faculty collective bargaining and governance in general. Professor Mason's thorough survey of the literature provides a particularly helpful framework within which to view the collective bargaining process.

Next, Ellis Katz, who was intimately involved in the campaign to establish collective bargaining at Temple University, reports on the circumstances that prompted his colleagues to opt for representation by a bargaining agent. Professor Katz argues the case for trade-unionism among faculty members.

The next essay emanates from the other side of the bargaining table. Caesar Naples, chief employee relations officer for negotiations and contract administration at the State University of New York, develops a provocative thesis: faculty bargaining will give administrators substantially more *de facto* control over academic policy-making than they now customarily possess.

Following that, Robert Carr, an eminent authority on faculty collective bargaining, examines current developments concerning a critically important aspect of negotiations—the changing composition of faculty bargaining units as determined by the National Labor Relations Board and state public employment relations boards.

Finally, I treat several emerging issues, including the role of students in faculty collective bargaining and the as yet unsuccessful search for fresh approaches to faculty unionism which might improve upon the industrial model.

This issue stems from a session on faculty collective bargaining at the 1973 annual meeting of the American Political Science Association in New Orleans, where I asked my colleagues to address the topics presented here. I am particularly grateful to Allen P. Sindler of the University of California, Berkeley, distinguished student of American government and university governance, for affording me the opportunity to organize that session. My colleagues and I hope that this issue of *New Directions for Higher Education* will enable the reader to encounter the unionized university with sharp insights and increased sensitivity to the nuances of this dynamic and controversial topic.

Jack H. Schuster
Issue Editor

*Perspective on the controversies that have
erupted over academic collective bargaining and
its impact on academic government.*

faculty unionism and university governance

henry l. mason

The governing body of a university makes no attempt
to control its professors and instructors as if they were
its servants. By practice and tradition, the members of
the faculty are masters and not servants.—Justice Car-
dozo (quoted by McHugh, 1971, p. 70).

The developments of the next several years under faculty collective bargaining should indicate whether collective bargaining will alter the traditional role of the
faculty or whether the faculty will alter the traditional
concept of collective bargaining.—Vice-Chancellor Bernard Mintz, The City University of New York (1971,
p. 124).

the shared authority model

Academicians have not, as yet, done much serious work on
governmental processes in academe. There is general agreement—not
just in academic novels—that universities constitute a political sys-

1

tem; the decisions which universities make for their "internal life" clearly reflect the kinds of political judgments and jurisdictions normally exercised by governmental bodies of or within modern states (see, for example, Moodie and Eustace, 1971, p. 295). But there is an amazing paucity of systematic thought, let alone empirical research, on conceptual models of academic decision making.

A sort of consensus has developed on the merits of the so-called shared authority model, a model which has been depicted in the *Statement on Government of Colleges and Universities* (1966). The legitimacy of this landmark Statement is supported by its adoption in 1966 as the official governance model of the American Association of University Professors and by its endorsement, somewhat more hesitantly perhaps, by the American Council on Education and the Association of Governing Boards of Universities and Colleges. The 1966 Statement posits that decision making in the university requires *both* the full-time efforts of professionalized bureaucrats or bureaucratized professionals (a component called, rather misleadingly, the administration) and the part-time but intensive governance participation of the faculty, with lesser roles for the trustees and the students. As Sanford Kadish, former AAUP president, has observed, the model put forth by the 1966 Statement exists nowhere perfectly, "but it has tended to be the mode of *rapprochement* between bureaucracy and professionalism in institutions of higher education to which faculties have traditionally aspired" (1968, p. 163). Even if some members of administrations and boards of trustees have not seemed overly enthusiastic in their "aspiration" to this model, many of them have applied its principles in their actual governance relationships with faculties—as much conventional wisdom and some empirical investigation suggest. (See, for example, Deegan and Mortimer, 1970; Mason, 1972, pp. 91-174; McConnell and Mortimer, 1971; and Mortimer, 1970.)

The shared authority model presents an aspiration. Yet its supporters also claim for it inherent, realistic applicability because of what the 1966 Statement calls the "variety and complexity" of the tasks performed by academic institutions and the "inescapable interdependence" particularly between the administration and the faculty, and between these two groups and the trustees. Certain crucial tasks—such as teaching, evaluating student performance, curriculum planning, and deciding on faculty status—can most competently be performed by the faculty; other important decision-making situations require the competence or full-time effort of the administration. Shared authority is said to be the only effective basis for operating an academic enterprise; all other ways would produce unprofessional, illegitimate results, at least in the long run.

other models

Acceptance of the shared authority model leads to distrust of certain other models. The *hierarchical model* of the governmental bureaucracy, the business corporation, or the armed forces is considered completely out of place where the most sensitive and crucial decisions—those pertaining to teaching and research—are made essentially "down" at the level of the "assembly line" by the individual professor in his classroom, study, or laboratory. As Logan Wilson, the long-time president of the American Council on Education, once put it, the differences between the professor and the administrator are "more analogous to those between the infantry officer and the artillery officer than to those between the captain and the general" (quoted in Mason, 1972, p. 3. Note also Corson, 1960, pp. 129, 130; and Clark, 1961, pp. 300-301). In the hierarchical structure the "higher-up" commands legitimately because he is assumed to know more about the organization's business: this is nowhere less true than in the university. Equally inappropriate for academic decision making, from the point of view of shared authority, is the *interest group or political model.*

> Most issues of university policy are questions requiring qualitative judgments rooted in values and principles. Such questions cannot readily be broken down into component units over which highly politicized interest groups can bargain. . . . To pursue university policy as a task of trading off the interests of competing groups . . . [obscures] the special character of a university [Foote, Mayer, and Associates, 1968, p. 18].

As Dallas Sands observed, it is "invidious" to reach academic decisions "on the balance of partisan self-interest . . . rather than by the balance of reason and persuasion"—as if academic components "were political constituencies to which the one-man one-vote rule should apply" (1971, p. 175). Not only the political but more specifically the *democratic model* is seen as being in conflict with shared authority. The Berkeley faculty study stressed this point:

> A university is not a natural democracy composed of members each of whom is distinguished by an equal claim to power; it is a highly artificial community deliberately arranged so that the educational relationships among the members constitute the starkest kind of contrast to relationships based on power. . . . Qualitative distinctions . . . [must be made constantly] not only concerning ideas, but also concerning individual achievements [Foote, Mayer, and Associates, 1968, p. 80].

In many important respects the academic decision-making process of the shared authority model does not resemble a democratic system, and mere majoritarianism seldom has any place in it.

It is hardly surprising that shared authority should appear in very crass contradiction indeed to the *collective bargaining model* where employers and employees bargain and clash in conflicts of interests which are frequently irreconcilable and can only be resolved by contests of force, "brute" or otherwise. Basic "production point" arguments are easily marshalled to prove the "regressive" aims of labor unions as compared to faculty aims under shared authority.

> Whoever heard of the union in industry helping to choose . . . the president, the plant superintendent, or the shop foreman? Do unions in industry decide what should be produced, what raw materials should be bought, or what processes should be used? The traditional structure of the university is that faculty members have a role . . . that reaches far beyond even the wildest dreams of the most radical unions [Clyde Summers, as quoted by Sands, 1971, p. 156].

Nevertheless, it is the collective bargaining model which currently is providing the most serious challenge to shared authority. Has the economic recession in academe, the sudden transition from the fat years to this period of Nixonian privation, simply led to the instant borrowing of an "alien" model which apparently has worked well in private industry and even in public employment? Or has the model of shared authority been found to lack effectiveness on so many campuses that a drastic change of model became necessary? Or is it assumed now that the two contrasting models can, after all, be applied at the same time and place without overly great injury to the basic principles and strategies of either shared authority or collective bargaining?

collective bargaining and shared authority: doubts

A study of university government published in 1967 expressed the fear that the shared authority model might not survive if faculties were to resort to collective bargaining. The authors felt that the attempt to divide campus jurisdictions between the bargaining agent and organs such as university senates would prove "unstable over time," with a steady expansion of union influence and decline of the senate. More and more issues would be removed from the sphere of shared authority and appear at the bargaining table (*Faculty Participation in Academic Governance*, 1967, pp. 20-24, 65). William F. McHugh criticized the notion, "still in currency," that academic and economic issues were easily distinguishable and that unions and traditional governance organs could exist side by side: "this seems an unrealistic analysis" in light of experience (1971, p. 84). Dallas Sands found "brute strength, whether it be economic, political, or any other kind, . . . oddly out of place in that human institution which is or ought to be uniquely committed to the rule of reason" (1971, p. 173).

Matthew Finkin provided a first survey of the actual impact of collective bargaining on traditional university government in other than two-year colleges. He concluded, in 1971, that it was too early to predict whether the shared authority model could survive where collective bargaining was introduced, but he hoped the outlook might become more optimistic as more and more "mature" academic institutions entered the collective bargaining sphere. A year later Finkin studied one such institution, the City University of New York (CUNY), and found that collective bargaining as such did not "mandate" the undermining of the academic character of CUNY—but again, he did not rule out such undermining if the contract negotiations then taking place were to take the wrong turn (1971, pp. 149-162; 1972, p. 17).

The AAUP's attitude toward collective bargaining has been termed "schizoid" (Wollett, 1971, p. 7). In 1972, a prestigious *minority* of its National Council—including Association president Kadish, first first vice-president Robert Webb, and Committee A chairman William Van Alstyne—warned that the "industrial model" would thrust out the "academic model," that with collective bargaining traditional organs of faculty government would disappear and the holiest principles of the Association would become mere bargaining counters (Kadish, Van Alstyne and Webb, 1972). Before 1966 many members of the AAUP probably considered collective bargaining to be incompatible with its principles.

collective bargaining and shared authority: optimism

Since 1966 the majority in the AAUP increasingly, and after 1972 overwhelmingly, has seen no contradiction between collective bargaining and the governance principles of the Association. At the 1972 annual meeting in New Orleans, the incoming president and first vice-president, Walter Adams and Carl Stevens, led an enthusiastic convention majority toward a strong collective bargaining stance. Stevens emphasized that the shared authority model had not been permitted to operate by the administrations of a great number of institutions; therefore collective bargaining, rather than undermining the 1966 Statement, should be used to shore up its ideals. Faculty members must use the leverage of collective bargaining to achieve de facto and de jure recognition of their right to share effectively in the making of decisions which belong in the domain of their own professional competence. If AAUP chapters refuse to engage in collective bargaining, numerous faculty members will in effect be denied their best chance to participate in sound and effective academic governance. Besides, as Stevens insisted—and this second point can perhaps stand up regardless of the merits of the previous one—the quality of a contract, with respect to governance and other matters, depends on the aegis under which it is negotiated. The AAUP's long-standing concern with the quality of academic government must now be extended to those situations where governance rights are achieved by collective bargaining; new policy positions must be developed to adjust collective bargaining norms and procedures to the model of the 1966 Statement (Stevens, 1972).

Accordingly, the AAUP's Committee N on Representation of Economic and Professional Interests, in its policy statement on collective bargaining of October 1972, put much emphasis on governance problems; two of the four advisory points for chapters which achieve representation status stress their obligation to establish structures and procedures which provide for faculty participation in accordance with the 1966 Statement (AAUP, 1972). Even if some consider the question of the compatibility between unionizing and shared authority as unresolved, the AAUP is evidently not willing to leave academic collective bargaining to its two main competitors. The AFT (American Federation of Teachers, AFL-CIO) and the NEA (National Education Association) draw most of their experience from elementary and secondary schools, and, at best, two-year community colleges; "as a result, the AFT and NEA policies toward the scope of bargaining in higher education are virtually identical to their policies formulated for elementary and secondary schools" (Moskow, 1971, p. 35). Because of its "feel" for higher education, the AAUP may have a chance to beat the AFT and NEA in academe if it can present a unified and determined collective bargaining stance.

Impetus for Bargaining. Two factors, at least, are currently making faculties less optimistic about shared authority and therefore more eager to try the union model—the making of systems-wide decisions away from the campus and the new "managerial" techniques on the campus. The 1966 Statement, in spite of a recently added footnote acknowledging the growth of "autonomous statewide bodies superordinate to existing Boards of Trustees" and declaring that the objectives and practices of the 1966 Statement are equally applicable to these bodies (see p. 336 of the *AAUP Bulletin* for Autumn 1972), does not really contribute much to the increasingly urgent problem of securing faculty participation in academic decision making at statewide levels. As Donald Wollett remarked, "the establishment of statewide systems of higher education has had a sharp impact on the role of the faculty on the individual campus, even on those campuses which have well functioning procedures for faculty representation." Consequently, many faculty members "have become restive over the loss of control that they once thought was theirs" (Wollett, 1971, p. 8: note also Mason, 1972, p. 67).

A second kind of frustration, also affecting the faculty's view of the feasibility of shared authority, has resulted from the introduction of new managerial techniques on the campus. As described convincingly by Rourke and Brooks, the computer has upset a traditional balance of communication flow and control between faculty and administration; the department, that primary locale of faculty power, especially has suffered (1966, pp. 37-38, 108).

In any event, collective bargaining is in the air. Formal recognition has been granted to faculty bargaining units on more than three hundred campuses, involving approximately 15 percent of the nation's faculty members. Hundreds of other institutions, including an increasing number of four-year colleges and universities, are preparing for certification of faculty representation. Some twenty states have passed enabling legislation which compels, or permits, public institutions to recognize duly elected faculty bargaining representatives. In 1970 the National Labor Relations Board announced its readiness to assume jurisdiction over collective bargaining in most private institutions.

Peaceful Coexistence? A veritable "domino" effect is evident, in spite of several setbacks for the unions. Besides, the public pronouncements of "the other side" are by no means offensive to AAUP-ers imbued with shared authority doctrines. For example, Israel Kugler of the AFT in 1968 urged unions and senates to complement one another: "rather than being opposed to senates, the Federation seeks to achieve full, not merely advisory, authority for senates." An NEA leader in New Jersey insisted that unions and senates do not compete "but serve different functions," and the NEA agent at CUNY was found "sincere" in his attempt to incorporate many senate functions into the contract (Mortimer and Lozier, 1972, pp. 21, 26).

Collective bargaining is in the air, and commentators are reaching the comfortable conclusion that "blanket statements about the inevitability of conflict between coexisting senates and bargaining agents" are out of place; Mortimer and Lozier (p. 3) conclude that "very likely, incompatibility will be the result in some institutions; in others, the two organizations may find convenient and compatible accommodations which will strengthen the effectiveness of each group." Collective bargaining and shared authority "do not have to be an either-or dichotomy"; higher education may "utilize collective bargaining rather than be utilized by it" (Mintz, 1971, p. 124).

Faculties and administrations could well succeed in developing new approaches to collective bargaining which would modify some of the more crassly unacademic aspects of an industrial model of unionization. Dallas Sands mentions the possibility, for example, of "joint bargaining committees constituted on the basis of proportional representation," rather than giving exclusive status to the agent who happens to win a majority vote, however narrow; he also suggests that a contract should not necessarily have to run for a specified period, so that the periodic "convulsions" around the time of

contract renewal might be avoided. Sands calls for "experimentation" to discover what kind of collective bargaining works best in
universities and for other-than-conventional legislation to provide
"alternative means in lieu of economic warfare" for bringing the
bargaining parties together—with specific guarantees for the faculty's rights of shared authority (1971, pp. 169-171, 176). And Dex-
ter L. Hanley suggested a "professional negotiating team" consisting
of faculty members *and* administrators (1971).

In many institutions the financial plight of the faculty may
be so desperate, interferences with academic freedom so common,
and conditions of academic governance so primitive that nothing
meaningful would be sacrificed by applying the union model. Yet in
a great number of other institutions the question of whether shared
authority principles can be adapted to the principles and conditions
of collective bargaining remains highly unsettled.

In the following section, some governance-related problems
will be discussed which have become evident in the brief experience
with collective bargaining: first, the dependence of a unionizing faculty on such outside agents as labor relations boards or arbitrators;
second, the incorporation of governance provisions into contracts,
and the attempts in the contracts to resolve jurisdictional conflicts
between governance organs, "management" rights, and union authority; finally, and very briefly, such aspects of collective bargaining as the agency shop, the strike, and relations with the "consumers"—the students.

determining the bargaining unit

One of the more crucial, yet often quite subjective, decisions
facing a campus that is undertaking collective bargaining is how to
determine the membership of the bargaining unit. Should the unit
consist only of full-time faculty members, or should part-time faculty also be included even if their primary economic and other concerns are off campus? Should there be only teachers and researchers
in the unit, or should librarians and all kinds of "professional support staff" be added? Should the bargaining unit be confined to one
campus, or should it contain an entire system—a system which
might consist of community colleges, technological and agricultural
institutions, four-year colleges, and graduate and professional
schools? Should certain administration personnel, such as assistant
and associate deans, be in the unit, and, more important, should

department chairmen be included? Finally, should some faculties— for example, law or medicine—be authorized to remain outside the regular bargaining unit?

Such questions of unit determination are, in the final instance, decided by an agency outside the university—usually the National Labor Relations Board (NLRB) for private institutions and a state labor relations board for public institutions. Yet, as McHugh notes (1971, p. 62), "the size and composition of the bargaining units can often be decisive in terms of which organization will win recognition or certification." A labor relations board, by deciding on a certain type of unit, can make it virtually impossible for an AAUP chapter, for example, to become the bargaining unit, and may, in effect, throw an election to the AFT or NEA or some other competitor. For example, the New York Public Employment Relations Board (PERB) initially ruled that at the City University of New York (CUNY) there should be two bargaining units, one for the permanent faculty and one for the part-time faculty. During the elections in 1968 and 1969 an "inhouse" agent (later affiliating with the NEA) won representation for the full-time faculty and the AFT for the part-timers. As McHugh observed, if PERB had determined to have only one unit at CUNY, the AFT would probably have been victorious; by the division of the unit, another agent was given a chance (1971, p. 79). (Since then, the two bargaining units at CUNY have merged into a single AFT-NEA unit—the Professional Staff Congress.)

Professional Support Staff. The AAUP has traditionally limited its membership to full-time teachers and researchers and, more recently, certain librarians—but excluded what is currently referred to as "professional support staff," such as student counselors, financial aid specialists, admissions officers, laboratory assistants, and technicians. In one case—the system of the State University of New York (SUNY)—the category of professional support staff amounted to fully 27 percent of the bargaining unit (Mortimer and Lozier, 1972, p. 9). Arguments against including this category of staff in the bargaining unit were summed up by McHugh: such persons are not subject to the peer group-determined procedures for appointment, promotion, and tenure as are faculty; their work hours generally require a regularized eight-hour work day with some kind of supervisory system; they do not participate in the community of an academic department, the crucial decision-making unit of the faculty, and they have not played a role in the other governance structures of the faculty; finally, the principles and protection of academic freedom have not been applied to them.

Nevertheless, PERB ruled for SUNY that the professional support staff should be in the same bargaining unit as the professors, finding that "they share a community of professional interest with the rest of the permanent staff because they are engaged in directly supportive activities that are clearly and closely associated with the function of teaching or research." Although the board admitted that the question was "not free from doubt," it felt obliged to apply its basic policy "not to fragment employees having a basic community of interest." Differences between professors and professional support staff did not "constitute conflicts of interest that would prevent meaningful and effective negotiations"; the differences in working conditions did not have the same significance as those involving, for example, "professionals and rank-in-file employees" (McHugh, 1971, pp. 75-76).

PERB's decision on the SUNY bargaining unit may be destined to be the rule rather than the exception: "the definition of bargaining units appears to be pushing toward a homogenization of regular faculty with ... professional non-teaching staff," although contrary decisions were also noted (McHugh, 1971, pp. 76-77). At its 1972 annual meeting, the AAUP duly voted to grant membership henceforth to all those nonacademic professionals who had been included in a bargaining unit as a result of labor relations board rulings.

Not clear, as yet, is the impact of this kind of homogenization on traditional governance relationships. Will a homogenized bargaining unit still care for the kinds of principles which the 1966 Statement tries to establish? Even long-time, full-time faculty members have had difficulties in appreciating their own role in the shared authority model, as Dykes so clearly points out (1968). Mortimer and Lozier foresee the development of "new alliances" in the university as a result of the presence of faculty and support personnel in the bargaining unit (1972, p. 11). Will these new alliances depend on a consensus quite unrelated to the norms of the 1966 Statement?

Department Chairmen and Deans. Fortunately, some aspects of unit determination by labor relations boards appear to be strongly supportive of traditional governance practices. Mortimer and Lozier analyzed contracts in four-year institutions and found that department chairmen were generally included in the bargaining unit, although they were excluded in most of the community colleges; "this seems to be consistent with the hierarchical structure of many two-year colleges where the department chairman tends to be viewed as a representative of the administration" (1972, pp. 11-12). The heart of faculty participation in university government, the department, cannot function properly with the chairman as agent of "management"; surely, such a role would upset all the traditional relationships and balances in a faculty member's daily life in academe. Mortimer and Lozier, quite rightly, call for the appointment of "department stewards" in those institutions where the chairmen have to become agents of the administration (1972, p. 13), but evidently the labor relations boards are not pushing in that direction.

The New York board (PERB), in the SUNY case, also decided to keep associate and assistant deans within the bargaining unit, against the wishes of the AFT as well as the AAUP. The board argued, appropriately enough, that in a university setting, "since the faculty themselves aid in the development of policy and in certain instances may actually set policy," the managerial exclusion must be confined within narrow boundaries. "Given the faculty's role in faculty governance," only the highest administration officials should be excluded. As McHugh notes, each administration position should be individually reviewed "to ascertain the extent of supervisory responsibility and involvement in the policy decision-making process in the particular institution in question" (1971, p. 89). Apparently, PERB was aware of this responsibility.

Discrete Faculties. In other benchmark developments, the law school faculty at Fordham University was found "discrete" enough by the NLRB to comprise a separate unit, and this separate status was also granted the law school faculty at St. John's University in New York. (At St. John's the law faculty was excluded by the consent of the collective bargaining agent and the administration; at Fordham, the administration contested this exclusion.) If this type of ruling were to set a trend, the liberal arts faculties eventually might find themselves as the sole members of the central bargaining unit of the university, apart from all kinds of "discretely" separate units on the periphery—with not quite foreseeable consequences for problems of universitywide governance.

Superinstitutional Systems. Another problem of unit determination concerns institutions which form part of a system, usually statewide. In New York, PERB ruled that the appropriate unit for the huge SUNY system was at the statewide level; separate bargaining units for the individual campuses of SUNY would "balkanize" the system and would result in "a loose confederation of competing educational enterprises and therefore not a university at all." Besides, "almost all allegedly local issues will have serious statewide ramifications, either of an economic or policy nature." Similarly, the many campuses of the CUNY system, in New York City, were put into one bargaining unit. However, it is too early, according to McHugh, to see these pro-system decisions in New York as a definite trend in other states (1971, pp. 80-83). Nonbalkanization as an absolute good has been challenged by Finkin, who found one of the difficulties of collective bargaining at CUNY to be precisely the universal composition of the unit, "encompassing education from the community college through the graduate school" (1972, p. 16). In any case, balkanization fears did not seem to have been prominent when law schools were authorized to remove themselves from bargaining units. Since statewide systems, as was noted above, do present one of the major challenges to the feasibility of the shared authority model, statewide bargaining certainly looms as one possible answer—but at the kind of cost Finkin implies.

Impact of Labor Relations Boards. The NLRB promised in 1971 to take into account in its academic ruling "certain practices and organizational structures [in colleges and universities] which do not parallel the traditional practices and organizational structures in private industry." Moreover, the Board welcomed "the fruits of any research" in the academic area, for the use of its staff (see Mason, 1972, p. 25). It is evident that the NLRB and state labor boards will have considerable impact on academic governance through their powers to shape bargaining units; the quality of these configurations will be a reflection, partly, of their understanding of the academic scene. Since a good number of boards of trustees and administrations may not have consumed many "fruits of research," especially concerning shared authority, it may well be that a good number of their faculties may prefer final authority on specified campus matters to rest in a PERB rather than in their own boards or presidents. If off-campus authority can be legitimate in terms of its learning about the world of academe, then on many a campus it may become a welcome balancing force against those boards or administrations whose authority model is hierarchical rather than shared.

resort to arbitration

      Arbitrators, like the labor relations boards, are off-campus agents who through collective bargaining are destined to become influential in governance and other spheres of the university. Highly formalized grievance procedures, which include the possibility of final appeal to outside arbitrators, are among the most characteristic—and certainly most time-consuming—features of the unionized institution. Matthew Finkin made a first thorough survey of the arbitration of academic grievances in early 1973. While by no means all awards (decisions) were available to him, he did locate and study fifty-five awards concerning sixteen institutions; forty-one of these concerned matters of faculty status—traditionally one of the most crucial jurisdictions of faculties in university government.

      During the first three years of the contracts at CUNY, as many as 115 grievances on matters of faculty status were filed, and 60 percent of these were submitted to arbitration (Finkin, 1973, p. 2). Earlier, Vice-Chancellor Mintz had reported that during the first year of the contracts at CUNY some 130 grievances had reached the appeals level of the chancellor of the system; four awards had been handed down by arbitrators, and two additional cases were in "mid-hearing." According to Mintz, most of the grievances concerned job security—that is, the failure to reappoint temporary or nontenured faculty members—and involved charges of procedural violations against department chairmen and department committees who claimed to be exercising their "academic judgment." Apparently "the most grievance-laden" situation arose from "classroom observations and annual evaluations of faculty," practices imposed by the contracts with rather strict detail (1971, pp. 121-122).

      Numerous arbitration awards, evidently, will affect jurisdiction in matters of faculty status. According to the 1966 Statement, this jurisdiction is "primarily a faculty responsibility" and includes such decisions as "appointments, reappointments, decisions not to reappoint, promotions, the granting of tenure, and dismissal." This "primary" jurisdiction of the faculty is at the heart of a faculty's participation in campus governance, yet under arbitration it may not be maintained as a sphere where the faculty is predominant. Moreover, the arbitrators may be particularly unsuited for this particular task. Mintz (1971, pp. 121-122) expressed in strong terms his doubts about the arbitrators' substituting for professorial peer judgment:

Our arbitration experiences have been rather unfortunate in that one begins to have doubts about the wisdom of placing academic contract dispute adjudication in the hands of industry-oriented professionals. This statement is made with no intent to impugn either the expertise or integrity of any arbitrator, but rather to decry the difficulty and frustrations involved in explaining and justifying conventional and traditional procedures in the academic world to such arbiters. How does one explain that "failing of reappointment or tenure" is not synonymous with "dismissed" or "fired"? Or the consistency in a department's not recommending a man for reappointment, followed by the department chairman writing a fine letter of recommendation for such an unsuccessful candidate?

The CUNY agreements do specify that the arbitrators shall be "familiar with the customs, practices, nature and spirit of the academic community," but Mintz (1971, pp. 121-122) hints that not much will come of this because of "market thinness" and the procedural problems of challenging particular panel members. Also Finkin is worried about "the education of the arbitrator to the issues in the case and to the implications of his decision for the academic community," particularly because the earlier arbitral awards could become precedents for later cases, formally or informally. Finkin (1972, pp. 11-12) finds it "at least questionable" whether a body of arbitrators can develop competence similar to a body of colleagues who are "knowledgeable in academic values and sensitive to the implications of their decisions." Sands (1971, p. 172) wonders whether professors should not challenge any nonpeer judgment in the sphere of academic freedom, regardless whether it results from a decision by an administrator or an arbitrator; yet, in the end, he is prepared to accept carefully chosen and academically sensitive arbitrators as a reasonable means of resolving differences of opinion on questions of academic freedom.

In the CUNY contracts the attempt was made to keep decisions constituting "academic judgment" from the final appeals stage represented by binding arbitration; however, this provision was complicated, if not rendered meaningless, by the clause that academic judgment nevertheless could be taken to arbitration if the claim was made that the *procedure* in the academic judgment was arbitrary or discriminatory in areas such as appointment, reappointment, tenure, or promotion. The arbitrator should rule in such cases whether the grievance relates in effect to procedure rather than academic judgment, and he is specifically prohibited from substituting his judgment for the academic judgment.

Finkin wonders, rightly, whether this distinction between "procedural" and "academic" will provide a sufficiently precise standard to restrain the arbitrators (1973, p. 2). In his most recent draft, confirmation for his earlier doubts in this respect can be found. The procedure and academic judgment distinctions "*nevertheless require consideration of the underlying merits,*" and thus "it seems that arbitrators have brought to bear *their own reactions to the merits of these decisions* in deciding whether there was a true academic judgment or an abuse of procedure" (1972, p. 25; italics added). In at least two cases Finkin noted that the arbitrator had, in effect, "adopted as a standard for judgment the *reasonableness* of the department's standards for the qualification of its members." In another case the arbitrator undertook, quite openly, to determine the qualifications and competence of a faculty member.

In spite of one arbitrator's remarkable assertion that, "as every educator knows, the capability of a teacher is ascertainable by scientific measurement," Finkin wonders about "the competence of arbitrators to make determinations involving subtle matters of teaching, scholarship and colleagueship" (1973, pp. 21, 27). In the contract demands of the CUNY union, the whole concept of academic judgment by peer groups appears in an odd light. "Academic judgment" must be specifically defined for each occasion and "an analysis of each member of the department or program in a relative position must be made to determine the validity of academic judgment" (Finkin, 1972, p. 8). As academic judgment becomes as suspect as, let's say, discrimination, the arbitrator would seem to have innumerable openings for substituting his judgment for that of professorial peer groups.

It is certainly possible that effective restrictions on arbitrators' intrusions into primary faculty jurisdictions might be devised for contracts. For example, in the agreement at St. John's University (where the AAUP chapter is one of the bargaining agents) a wide range of peer judgments pertaining to faculty status appear to be excluded from grievance-arbitration procedures (Article X). Another AAUP contract, at Oakland University, has seemingly impressive restrictions on the arbitrator's authority. Properly structured, resort to arbitration does not necessarily lessen the autonomy of a faculty—particularly not, of course, in institutions where administrations have not heeded peer judgments in the past. Besides, faculty bodies themselves "are not wholly immune from arbitrariness, administrative pressure or ineptitude." Arbitration might be used to correct administration (and faculty!) abuse, while still leaving intact primary prerogatives of peer judgment (Finkin, 1973, pp. 4, 45-46).

The main task is to devise an arbitration system in which the arbitrator's personal value judgments of academic decisions, such as on faculty status, are minimized—or else a system in which the arbitrator is particularly close to the values of academicians. Finkin noted the totally absent, or at best cursory, references in awards to academic practices and to the "common law of the [academic] shop." He suggested a "national academic tribunal"—a standing body of academicians along the lines, perhaps, of the AAUP's Committee A—to substitute for ad hoc arbitration and to develop "consistent decisional law." Such a national tribunal would bring relief from the balkanization of inconsistent, often contradictory, decisions of many particular arbitrators working a system of what has been called "judicial roulette" (1973, pp. 44, 47-49).

incorporating the governance model

A notion still in currency is that academic and economic issues are easily distinguishable. It is believed in some quarters that the bargaining process will be confined to economic issues and that academic issues may be relegated to existing governance bodies such as faculty senates or councils and the like. Thus, the bargaining agent will have jurisdiction over economic issues and governance bodies will determine academic policies. In light of experience to date, however, this seems an unrealistic analysis since the scope of bargaining has encompassed both academic and policy issues customarily handled by faculty senates, as well as purely economic matter [McHugh, 1971, p. 84].

If, as McHugh believes, governance and economic issues are not easily distinguishable, it is essential to guarantee in the contract the functioning of the traditional governmental systems of the university, at the level of the department as well as at the college and universitywide levels. More specifically, it would be essential to include the norms of the shared authority model in any collective bargaining arrangement. This happened emphatically at St. John's University, where the 1966 Statement was formally incorporated in Article II of the contract.

But many of the current contracts do not seem to demonstrate much concern for incorporating governance clauses. An analysis of more than fifty agreements in community or junior colleges revealed, perhaps not surprisingly, "that only a minority contain provisions calling for formal faculty participation in decision-making concerning educational policy" (Wollett, 1971, p. 15). Moreover, a survey by Mortimer and Lozier of governance-related provisions in the contracts of ten four-year colleges similarly demonstrated little, if any, interest in upgrading or guaranteeing faculty participation along the lines of shared authority (1972, pp. 39-40).

Even some of the AAUP-related contracts, except at St. John's, seem vague in this respect, at least on paper. At Oakland University, existing constitutions and "practices" in the governance sphere "shall be continued," but they are not specifically incorporated into the contract; participation in committees appears as the only governance-related task of faculty members which is mentioned in the contract. The contract at Rutgers contains no preference whatever to governance, and neither does the one at Belleville Area College. At the University of Rhode Island there is reference to the University Manual, which remains "in full force and effect."

Jurisdictional Conflicts. The evidence on incorporation of governance norms is inconclusive. Where contracts appear more specific, conflict of jurisdiction clauses are even more specific—and generally seem to resolve any conflict in favor of the collective bargaining sphere rather than the governance sphere. For example, at St. John's, "the presently constituted" governance bodies—"e.g., the University Senate, faculty councils, departmental personnel and budget committees, etc."—shall continue to function, but only "provided that the actions may not directly or *indirectly* repeal, rescind or *otherwise modify* the terms and conditions of this Agreement" (Article II, par. 2.5, my emphasis).

This kind of elastic clause must be reconciled with the 1966 Statement, which is also part of the St. John's contract; it is difficult to imagine many governance actions which would not "modify" some of the contract's terms, at least "indirectly." Similarly, at Oakland University the guarantee for the not-to-be-"diminished" right to carry out "past practices" of governance is, in fact, specifically diminished: "in the event of conflict between such established rights, privileges, and responsibilities and the provisions of this Agreement, the terms of this Agreement shall be controlling" (Article XV).

Finkin mentions the demands of the union at CUNY, which "would explicitly prohibit the University Faculty Senate and other faculty governing bodies ... from engaging in any activities which include 'those areas and interests which fall within the domain of the Collective Bargaining Agent.' " Also, the university would be prohibited from financing or "agreeing with" a governance body with respect to any matter which "affects" or "impinges on" the contract. As Finkin concludes, "it is clear that under these demands internal faculty governing bodies will have jurisdiction over only those matters for which the bargaining agent chooses not to assert that *it* has jurisdiction." Given the interrelations between governance decisions and working conditions, the union could claim that "almost any matter falls within its 'domain' or 'impinges' on its rights." Thus, if the demands at CUNY were granted, faculty governance participation would be "at the sufferance of the bargaining agent" (1972, pp. 3-4, 10). Apparently, jurisdictional conflicts between the contract and governance organs will not be resolved in favor of the latter.

Management Rights. Another threat to the spirit, at least, of the 1966 Statement, particularly its attempt to balance the power of the various components, may result from the kinds of "management rights" clauses which appear frequently in collective bargaining agreements. Michael Moskow notes "the high incidence" of such clauses (1971, p. 51). At the University of Rhode Island, "management rights" include "the authority to manage and direct ... all the operations and activities of the University to the full extent authorized by law"—and the "employees" must attend all faculty and department meetings (Article II).

Another AAUP contract, at Ashland College (Ohio), stipulates that "the management and control" of the institution "in all its phases and details" and "the direction and control of the employees" shall remain vested in the college, except as limited by the express terms of the contract, which does incorporate a seemingly sound faculty senate. This senate document reflects the kind of looseness not untypical of the spirit of the 1966 Statement; the exclusive tightness of the management-rights clause contrasts with the looser provisions of the senate document in ways not so easily reconciled with the 1966 Statement—and certainly not advantageous for the faculty's side of the power balance.

Similarly, the AAUP contract at the New York Institute of Technology strongly emphasizes all kinds of supposed management rights—"to direct" the faculty, "to control" the operation of the Institute, "to introduce" new methods and programs of teaching, and so on—relieved by the promise that "AAUP governance guidelines" will be followed. This kind of language again suggests a weak obligation in the shared authority sphere as compared to the incisiveness of the management rights. At St. John's University, where the 1966 Statement is part of the contract, there is reference to "the desirability of generally resting final authority in the Administration, as *specified therein* [that is, in the 1966 Statement]" (Article II, par. 2.4., my italics)—which is not really what the 1966 Statement specifies at all in terms of its norms, principles, or possible applications.

Could it be that some of the unionizing institutions are, in effect, heading for an initial compromise between "management" and "employees" under which the faculty gains power in the economic sphere and the administration preserves a kind of supremacy in the governance sphere which the 1966 Statement certainly does not envisage? As more experience is gained with collective bargaining, faculties may recover some of the management rights. Of course, this discussion on incorporation of governance provisions was based on paper clauses in contracts; the reality on a campus may be quite different—and more encouraging for governance rights.

by-products of unionizing

Certain apparently inherent by-products of collective bargaining, with obvious impact on academic governance, will be mentioned very briefly—the need for exclusive representation and at least an agency shop; the appropriateness of the strike as an instrument of faculty power; and the consequences for the student consumers.

The Necessity of Exclusive Representation. In 1969 the AAUP insisted that a chapter which engages in collective bargaining could *not* require any person to become a member of or make a financial contribution to the Association as a condition of his enjoying the benefits of representation. As Sands observes, if a professor objects to the principle or practice of collective bargaining in his university "it arguably would violate his academic freedom to compel him to participate in or be identified with such activity." At the same time, he wonders whether the arguments for some kind of restricted shop—closed, union, or agency—are really "less relevant or substantial" for professors than for others engaged in collective bargaining. Sands concludes that in order to counterbalance the strength of management, at least an agency shop—whereby all those included in the bargaining unit, union and nonunion members alike, pay dues, or fees, to the union—will be required. He contends that "regular use of collective bargaining . . . would involve a much more continuous kind of service than the Association [AAUP] has rendered . . . heretofore; it, therefore, might be reasonable for the bargaining agent to claim a fee from nonmembers for their proportionate share of the cost of such services" (1971, pp. 166-167).

The agency shop will probably have to come, although in many states its legality is still undetermined. At CUNY, approximately two-thirds of the regular faculty are union members; the remainder are "freeloaders" who do not pay their annual contribution of $120, yet enjoy the benefits of the highest-paid university system in the United States. At some other unionized campuses the proportion of union members is even lower—at SUNY, for example, considerably lower. The doctrine of "exclusivity"—only one certified collective bargaining agent per unit of faculty—has been sustained in the state statutes and in academic contracts (McHugh, 1971, p. 83).

The consequence has been intense competition among the various affiliates of NEA, AFT, AAUP, and local and statewide groups. A majority of votes decides, and the stakes of winning a campus are extremely high, particularly in this initial unionizing period. The resulting "political atmosphere," as Mortimer and Lozier call it (1972, p. 19), is bound to have a profound effect on all kinds of relationships in the university, including governance. What comes to mind, once again, is the delicate nature of the balance and consensus prescribed in the 1966 Statement; a campus where rival unions must continuously appeal to the masses of voters of the faculty component may not be in the mood for either balance or consensus.

The Strike. With respect to the strike, the AAUP (1972) is again on the side of the "angels," as yet:

It is the policy of the Association (with which chapters should comply whether or not they are acting in a representative capacity) to call or support a faculty strike or other work stoppage only in extraordinary situations which so flagrantly violate academic freedom or the principles of academic government, or which are so resistant to rational methods of discussion, persuasion, and conciliation, that faculty members may feel impelled to express their condemnation by withholding their services, either individually or in concert with others. It should be assumed that faculty members will exercise their right to strike only if they believe that another component of the institution (or a controlling agency of government, such as a legislature or governor) is inflexibly bent on a course which undermines an essential element of the educational process.

In an earlier statement, still on the books, the AAUP specifically rules out strikes for the mere purpose of securing economic benefits. However, Sands concludes that strikes in universities need not be considered quite so extraordinary: the "essential" nature of a university's functioning "is insufficient to support a doctrinaire repudiation of the right to strike" (1971, p. 162). Merton Bernstein (1972) implies that strikes could not be outlawed in the university and might have salutary effects in spite of being "potentially very destructive weapons"; he prefers, and calls for campus experimentation with, limited types of strike—the "non-stoppage strike" and the "graduated strike."

Faculty strikes, obviously, would have great dramatic effect and would attract much attention if they were not used too often. In economic terms, in the short run at least, professors would certainly suffer more from a strike than their "employers," whose "profits" would hardly be affected by the strike. Yet the strike as a weapon is bound to be present on the unionized campus and its use—real, threatened, or at least implied by many precedents in the private and public sector—will at times provide leverage to faculties. (To date, the faculty strike has been used very sparingly, perhaps most notably at Oakland University in 1971.) The effect on university government, once again, will be particularly one of mood. If, in the professional milieu of the academic institution, things have gone so far that a strike must be maintained for more than one or two token days, the ensuing governance relationships between faculty and administration may at the end reflect shared authority—but not in the spirit of the 1966 Statement.

Impact on Students. What about the consumers on the campus, the students? Are they likely to be the hapless victims of Big Administration and Big Faculty? Will they too attempt to unionize, as did the teaching assistants at Wisconsin (Feinsinger and Roe, 1971) or as proposed by at least one student government? Frederic M. Brandes, executive director of the University Student Senate at CUNY, insists that "students must become part of the collective bargaining process." Academic senates, where students participate, will partly be replaced by collective bargaining—in which students are not yet represented. Therefore, "as members of the academic community of interest," students must share in the bargaining "to protect their education" (1973).

Whatever advances students had made through minor or more substantial inputs into the shared authority model may be rendered considerably less meaningful by faculty unionizing. Consumers outside the campus have not been organized effectively to counter collective bargaining, and university students may find getting together for this purpose even more difficult. The possible effects—on governance and all kinds of other academic purposes—of a second set of unions, representing the peculiarly complex (and numerous) component of the students, certainly stagger the imagination.

room for both unions and senates?

It is not difficult to foresee conflicts between unions and the traditional organs of university government. It would be convenient, obviously, in the unionized university simply "to establish by contract the faculty's independent authority"—to be exercised through the customary organs such as the department, the college assembly, or the senate. But many unions may prefer to by-pass and make impotent these customary structures, and to have *all* faculty authority exercised at the bargaining table and through the bargaining agent (Finkin, 1972, p. 9). At some institutions, at least, the union may be inclined to see the senate as an antiunion device, as a body somehow controlled by and subservient to the administration.

Such perceptions may be correct, or based on unfounded suspicions and erroneous impressions, but antagonism is produced in any case. Thus, a union is likely to become upset when the senate gets close to what the union considers its own jurisdiction, and the senate—as, for example, at CUNY—will protest vehemently when the union makes demands which include governmental jurisdiction previously exercised by the senate. The unionized campus may see rivalry between faculty members serving on, or supporting, the traditional structures and the unionists; of course, even more faculty energies are bound to be wasted by what could be virtually continuous electioneering on the part of competing unions.

Yet at some other institutions the union and the senate, and perhaps a nonunionizing AAUP chapter, may cooperate effectively. Apparently they did at CUNY for the purpose of keeping the chairmen within the bargaining unit. Particularly at the level of the state legislature, senate and union officers should find it worthwhile to collaborate. Some unions may sincerely try to keep out of the senate's domain, and serious jurisdictional conflicts may be avoidable. After all, many faculties may want to use both systems—the senate operating in the consultative-communal sphere where the components share authority through consensus; the union working its side particularly in the economic sphere through confrontation tactics and use of its muscle. The union could be generally useful as a much needed leverage device for the senate: a board may listen more respectfully to the senate if it knows that the union looms in the background, somewhere to the "left."

Senates and the other traditional structures of faculty participation in governance will have to maintain some kind of balance of strength with respect to the union. For the sake of this balance, greater faculty participation and loyalty will be needed to invigorate the shared authority model. Faculties at unionized campuses may no longer be able to afford their favorite tactic of civic withdrawal, of leaving the governance scene to a few (slightly suspect) activist-politicians among their colleagues and the administration. Senates and other faculty structures must stand on their own feet and not depend on the administration, let alone the union. Unfortunately, Dykes (1968, pp. 10, 41-42) was only too accurate in his analysis of many faculty members' neuroses, lethargy, and lack of civic spirit with respect to governance. Where senates are decaying in the unionized university, it may not be jealous unions or weak senate leaders that are to blame but the faculty itself because in its traditional ways it has failed to mobilize sufficient support for its governance structures.

The civic rebirth, if not birth, of the faculty may be the most crucial task for the nonunionizing AAUP chapter on a unionized campus. (If the AAUP is the bargaining agent, it is to be hoped that its devotion to the 1966 Statement will be sufficient to keep the senate alive, however weak and "Dykesian" the latter might be.) Traditional academic governance structures can survive even where the union is strong, but probably only if faculties change their civic ways. If they do, they may enjoy the cake provided by their contract, as well as the shared authority exercised by their senate.

references

American Association of University Professors. "Statement on Collective Bargaining." *AAUP Bulletin*, 1972, *58*, 423-424.

Bernstein, M. C. "Alternatives to the Strike." *AAUP Bulletin*, 1972, *58*, 404-412.

Brandes, F. M. *The Chronicle of Higher Education*, April 16, 1973, p. 12.

Clark, B. R. "Faculty Authority." *AAUP Bulletin*, 1961, *47*, 293-302.

Corson, J. J. *Governance of Colleges and Universities*. New York: McGraw-Hill, 1960.

Deegan, W. L., and Mortimer, K. P. *Faculty in Governance at the University of Minnesota*. Berkeley: Center for Research and Development in Higher Education, 1970.

Dykes, A. R. *Faculty Participation in Academic Decision Making*. Washington, D.C.: American Council on Education, 1968.

Faculty Participation in Academic Governance. Washington, D.C.: American Association for Higher Education, 1967.

Feinsinger, N. P., and Roe, E. J. "The University of Wisconsin, Madison Campus-TAA Dispute of 1969-70: A Case Study." *Wisconsin Law Review*, Vol. 1971, No. 1, 229-274.

Finkin, M. W. "Academic Implications of the Bargaining Demands of the Professional Staff Congress (AFT-NEA) in the City University of New York." Unpublished manuscript, August 29, 1972.

Finkin, M. W. "The Arbitration of Professional Grievances." Unpublished manuscript, 1973.

Finkin, M. W. "Collective Bargaining and University Government." *AAUP Bulletin*, 1971, *57*, 149-162.

Foote, C., Mayer, H., and Associates. *The Culture of the University: Governance and Education*. San Francisco: Jossey-Bass, 1968.

Hanley, D. L. "Issues and Models for Collective Bargaining in Higher Education." *Liberal Education*, 1971, *57*.

Kadish, S. H. "The Strike and the Professoriate." *AAUP Bulletin*, 1968, *54*, 160-168.

Kadish, S. H., Van Alstyne, W. W., and Webb, R. K. "The Manifest Unwisdom of the AAUP as a Collective Bargaining Agency: A Dissenting View." *AAUP Bulletin*, 1972, *58*, 57-61.

Mason, H. L. *College and University Government*. New Orleans: Tulane University, 1972.

McConnell, T. R., and Mortimer, K. P. *The Faculty in University Governance*. Berkeley: Center for Research and Development in Higher Education, 1971.

McHugh, W. F. "Collective Bargaining with Professionals in Higher Education: Problems in Unit Determinations." *Wisconsin Law Review*, Vol. 1971, No. 1, 55-90.

Mintz, B. "The CUNY Experience." *Wisconsin Law Review*, Vol. 1971, No. 1, 112-124.

Moodie, G. C., and Eustace, R. "British Universities as Political Systems." *Political Studies*, 1971, No. 1, 124.

Mortimer, K. P. *Academic Government at Berkeley: The Academic Senate.* Berkeley: Center for Research and Development in Higher Education, 1970.

Mortimer, K. P., and Lozier, G. G. "Collective Bargaining: Implications for Governance." *Center for the Study of Higher Education Report No. 17.* University Park: The Center, The Pennsylvania State University, 1972.

Moskow, M. H. "The Scope of Collective Bargaining in Higher Education." *Wisconsin Law Review*, Vol. 1971, No. 1, 33-54.

Rourke, F. E., and Brooks, G. E. *The Managerial Revolution in Higher Education.* Baltimore: Johns Hopkins, 1966.

Sands, C. D. "The Role of Collective Bargaining in Higher Education." *Wisconsin Law Review*, Vol. 1971, No. 1, 150-176.

Statement on Government of Colleges and Universities. *AAUP Bulletin*, 1966, *52*, 375-379.

Stevens, C. M. "A Statement in Support of the Council's Position." *AAUP Bulletin*, 1972, *58*, 54-57.

Wollett, D. H. "The Status and Trends of Collective Negotiations for Faculty in Higher Education." *Wisconsin Law Review*, Vol. 1971, No. 1, 2-32.

Henry L. Mason is chairman of the Department of Political Science at Tulane University and currently a visiting professor at the University of Amsterdam, where he is studying university government in Dutch and German universities. He directed the project on university government for the American Association of University Professors in 1968-1969 which led to his College and University Government: A Handbook of Principle and Practice *(Tulane University, 1972). Having held military and political intelligence positions in Europe and the United States and with a general interest in international politics, he has also published books on* The Purge of Dutch Quislings *(1952),* The European Coal and Steel Community *(1955);* Toynbee's Approach to World Politics *(1959); and* Mass Demonstrations Against Foreign Regimes *(1965).*

Advocacy of faculty unionization and alliance with the national labor movement, illustrated with a case study.

faculty stakes in collective bargaining: expectations and realities

ellis katz

Both faculty members and college administrators in large numbers have expressed surprise at the spread of collective bargaining in higher education. Although most of them have now come to recognize the inevitability of collective bargaining, many still cling to the hope that unionization will not disturb that traditional web of subtle relationships that exists in academe. They commonly warn against the creation of rigid governance structures which would prevent American higher education from meeting the challenges of the future. And most of all they are cautious, perplexed about how to maintain professional demeanor and status in this new setting.

My thesis is that those who are surprised, doubtful, and cautious are wrong. The forces that threaten higher education come primarily from outside the academy, and collective bargaining is a positive response to those threats—an attempt to preserve certain important values in the face of escalating external pressures. But these, of course, are conclusions, and before I attempt to justify them, I wish to clarify both the limitations and biases of this essay.

First, it should be obvious that the faculty of American higher education is not a homogeneous group. Included are young men and women who worry about raising families and meeting bills, members of religious orders who have renounced these worldly concerns, and wealthy, aristocratic full professors who can enjoy the pleasures of an academic life without economic concern. Also, faculty members work in a multitude of environments: small, rural liberal arts colleges; marginal state teachers colleges; burgeoning public and private universities. Furthermore, given the uneven growth of colleges and universities, there may be great diversity among the faculty of a single institution. Thus, it is altogether impossible to speak of a single faculty interest or stake in collective bargaining; obviously, no individual can claim to speak for all faculty.

In fact, I suppose that I cannot claim to speak for the faculty at Temple University. In December 1972, Temple held a collective bargaining election in which the American Association of University Professors (AAUP) won the right to bargain for the faculty and certain nonteaching professionals following a heated contest with both the American Federation of Teachers (AFT) and the National Education Association (NEA). I was the co-chairman of the AFT Local 2253 at Temple from 1970 until that election, and I assure you that during that time I obtained an extensive education about the attitudes of faculty members toward collective bargaining.

In addition to that personal experience, admittedly subject to bias, I base my conclusions on two other sources of data. First, there exists an extensive literature on higher education, on the history and sociology of the labor movement, and, more recently, on collective bargaining in higher education. Unfortunately, there have been no successful attempts to synthesize the concepts from these three areas. What is lacking is an essential perspective: a view of the rise of faculty collective bargaining in relation to changes in the economic, political, and cultural setting of higher education. Most studies of collective bargaining in higher education are concerned only with its impact on internal relationships. Also, most commentary on collective bargaining has been proffered by advocates—usually administrators—whose model of university governance hardly corresponds to my reality. In any case, the appropriate literature is surprisingly inadequate; it is unsystematic, biased, and, I think, largely inaccurate. Additionally, I have benefited from survey data on the attitudes of the Temple faculty toward collective bargaining.*

Finally, I make no claim to neutrality in these matters. I am both a social scientist and a socialist. From this position, two things follow. First, as I suggested above, it seems to me that choices within higher education are as much influenced by external forces as they are by decision-making processes within a university. While internal dynamics are important in understanding why a faculty turns to collective bargaining, it is at least equally important to explore an array of external political and economic developments. For example, it is probably true that the contemporary reevaluation of tenure is more a consequence of scarce economic resources than of any purely internal concern with the quality of the faculty. (See, for example, Walter P. Metzger [1973, pp. 93-160], America's leading authority on tenure, who recently concluded that much of the contemporary opposition to tenure is based on the current economic situation in higher education.)

The second ramification of my socialist brand of social science is that I am a trade unionist who still maintains that the working class represents the best hope for progressive social change. Thus, I see faculty affiliation with organized labor as vital. At present, only the AFT offers that affiliation, though at this writing it seems likely that the AFT and the NEA will work out some form of national merger which will retain a labor affiliation. Furthermore, there is some reason to believe that even the AAUP might develop an accommodation with a merged AFT-NEA. Thus, while I strongly prefer the AFT's more militant stance, I believe that both the NEA and the AAUP will come to adopt militant trade union positions.

the rise of collective bargaining at temple

An examination of collective bargaining's emergence at Temple University will be instructive, for the aspirations and pressures at Temple are not unlike those at other large, public universities. Temple is located in North Philadelphia, at the center of the city's most recent full-scale urban riot. The university, now state-related, was founded in the latter part of the nineteenth century as a private

*For this data I am indebted to Professor Steven Petkov of Pennsylvania State University.

institution to help train impoverished young men for the ministry. Gradually, Temple sprouted a full range of undergraduate programs, drawing its student body from among the working and middle class of Philadelphia.

During the 1960s, Temple, like many American universities, underwent dramatic changes. First, it became a state-related university—which means that the state of Pennsylvania contributes about one-third of Temple's operating budget and appoints a third of its trustees. Second, Temple has recruited a research-oriented faculty, developed many graduate programs, and greatly expanded its physical facilities. Today, approximately forty thousand students are enrolled in a broad range of undergraduate, graduate, and professional degree programs. During 1972-1973, more than eight thousand graduate students were enrolled in two hundred different graduate degree programs—compared to probably fewer than one thousand students in no more than ten programs a decade earlier. Today Temple employs over fifteen hundred full-time faculty members, many of whom are young assistant professors first hired during the late 1960s.

The rapid growth of the university created several important schisms among the faculty, resulting in divisions of rank (untenured assistant professors and tenured professors); divisions by political ideology (on such issues as affirmative hiring programs, open admissions, and the appropriateness of political activity); divisions by professional orientations (teaching versus research); and divisions by salary (the actual range of salaries for full professors in 1971-1972 was $15,000 to over $29,000). In these characteristics, Temple is probably not much different from many other large universities. But these facts are important to bear in mind when considering the development of collective bargaining.

The move toward collective bargaining began during the summer of 1970. A group of young, progressive, mostly untenured faculty members held a series of meetings to discuss the role of intellectuals in American politics. They were frustrated with the continuation of the Vietnam War and with President Nixon's apparent lack of concern with important domestic problems. Most had participated in teach-ins, demonstrations, and various radical caucuses and now sought new forms of political activity.

Their meetings coincided with the passage by the state legislature of the Pennsylvania Employees Relations Act, which, beginning in October 1970, permitted collective bargaining by state employees. Initially their attention focused on unionization as a means of political influence. Then the group split over this issue: a minority maintained that trade unionism of necessity was reactionary, while the remaining members continued vigorously to pursue their interest in collective bargaining. Thus, the original impetus for bargaining, at least at Temple, sprang from the radical political activity by faculty members that characterized much of American politics during the late 1960s.

This embryonic group held a series of meetings with representatives of the AAUP, the AFT and the NEA. In light of their commitment to political action, it is not surprising that they decided to form an AFT local and seek to organize the faculty. In the fall of 1970, the group announced its presence, held a series of open meetings, and began an authorization card drive.

Events moved rapidly. Before long the leadership of the faculty senate endorsed collective bargaining, but suggested that the faculty remain independent of the AAUP, the AFT, and the NEA, thereby giving birth to a competing group. Made up largely of faculty members who had been at Temple prior to the dramatic changes of the 1960s, the Faculty Collective Bargaining Committee (FCBA) promptly began their own authorization card campaign. Finally, the local AAUP chapter, after polling its members, joined the race as well.

On June 3, 1971, the FCBA filed a petition with the Pennsylvania Labor Relations Board (PLRB) and hearings began in October 1971. The parties to the hearings were the FCBA, the AFT, the AAUP, the university administration, the faculty of the law school (which filed its own petition and sought recognition independent of the rest of the faculty), and the faculties of the dental and medical schools (who sought to remain outside the collective bargaining process altogether).

The principal issues at the hearings were these:

(1) Should the faculties of the schools of law, medicine, and dentistry be severed from the bargaining unit?

(2) Which nonteaching professional employees should be included within the bargaining unit?

(3) Should department chairmen be excluded from the bargaining unit as "supervisors" within the meaning of the state law?

(4) Should certain department heads in the library be excluded from the unit as "management" within the meaning of the law?

Though there was some initial disagreement among the various employee organizations, they negotiated among themselves and finally agreed that (1) the faculties of the law, medical, and dental schools should be excluded; (2) most of the nonteaching professional employees, except those at the Temple University Hospital, should be included; and (3) department chairmen and department heads from the library should be included.

The university administration contested the faculty groups' position on each of these issues. (No one had raised the issue of part-time employees and all agreed that they should not be included in the bargaining unit.) The PLRB hearings continued until the spring of 1972. At long last, during the summer of 1972, the Board issued its ruling. It favored the unified position of the employee organizations on all issues except one: the relationship of the department heads in the library to a bargaining unit was not resolved, but was left open for the AFT, AAUP, and FCBA to work out with the university administration.

Sharply Contested Race. Even before the hearings began, the three groups campaigned for the support of the faculty. All three sent out mailings, held informal luncheon meetings with small groups of faculty, and attempted to create campaign organizations at both the department and college level.

While the tactics of each were similar, their overall strategies were quite different. Each of the three, of course, had to construct a strategy to enable it, at a minimum, to qualify for the run-off election (between the top two groups) should it fail to win a majority in the initial election. The AFT had a substantial group of loyal and active followers. Its difficult challenge was to increase its support among that large segment of the faculty that had less knowledge about collective bargaining. Because the AFT had the most militant reputation, it had to convince the faculty that it was more than a "bread-and-butter" trade union. Consequently, the AFT waged an educational campaign, issuing thoughtful policy statements on a variety of important topics.

The situation of the AAUP was quite different. Its primary asset was a large membership and a reservoir of good will among almost all segments of the faculty. Its problem was to convince the faculty that it could be as effective in collective bargaining as it had been in protecting faculty interests by more traditional means. Confident that it could beat the AFT in a run-off election, the AAUP's dual goal was to prevent the AFT from obtaining a majority on the first ballot and to beat out the FCBA for second place.

The FCBA was saddled with the most difficult position. Starting as an independent organization, it gradually accepted financial and legal help from the National Education Association. During the last few weeks of the campaign, NEA organizers appeared on campus, leading to a rift between the NEA organizers and the original founders of the FCBA. The NEA, as a national organization, has a view of collective bargaining similar to that of the AFT. However, the local faculty leadership was considerably more conservative. Both the AFT and the AAUP attacked the FCBA/NEA arrangement and the faculty in general was confused about the nature of the organization.

Although opposition to any form of collective bargaining may have been widespread, there was no organized support for the "no bargaining" option which would also appear on the ballot. The AAUP made a strong effort to convince the faculty that the "no bargaining" option could not win, and that those who opposed collective bargaining were better off voting for the AAUP so as to prevent the AFT from winning. There is some evidence to indicate that this strategy worked for the AAUP.

The results of the first election, held in October 1972, were about as expected—an extremely close three-way finish. The AFT led with 328 votes, the AAUP had 303, and the FCBA mustered 280. One hundred eighty-seven voted against collective bargaining. In all, almost 80 percent of those eligible voted. And of those who did vote, more than 80 percent opted for some form of collective bargaining.

The run-off election was scheduled for the following month. The leadership of the defeated FCBA met with both the AFT and the AAUP. They decided to support the AFT. Some observers of this surprising decision have noted that beyond the great personal animosity between leaders of the FCBA and leaders of the AAUP, the FCBA leaders gradually had come to recognize the need for militant collective bargaining. In their view, the choice between the AFT and the AAUP was a choice between bargaining and essentially no bargaining. Indeed, analysis of Petkov's survey data indicates that many faculty members saw the choice in identical terms. In the run-off election between the AAUP and the AFT, the AAUP won handily. The vote was 626 to 437.

Cross-pressured Faculty the Key. Where did the AAUP's run-off strength come from? According to the survey data, about half of those who had supported the FCBA in the first election disregarded the recommendation of the FCBA leadership and now voted for the AAUP. Moreover, almost 90 percent of those who had voted against collective bargaining in the first election voted for the AAUP in the run-off.

It is important to understand the dynamics of the vote in order to grasp the complexity of the Temple faculty's decision to endorse collective bargaining. Though the following analysis is surely an oversimplification, the Temple faculty seemed to have been divided into three basic groups: those who strongly endorsed collective bargaining and voted for the AFT in both elections; those who strongly opposed collective bargaining and voted against bargaining in the first election and either did not vote or voted for the AAUP in the second election; and those who voted for collective bargaining, but with considerable reservation.

This last group, which had voted for either the FCBA or the AAUP in the first election and for the AAUP in the run-off, was clearly the largest. Surprisingly, examination of traditional categories such as tenure status, rank, salary, and academic discipline does not help to identify these voters. Rather, they seem to share certain psychological dimensions. On the one hand, they have strong commitments to "professionalism" and to the concerns of their respective academic disciplines. On the other hand, they tend to feel that they are underpaid: salary was ranked among their highest concerns. They were, in effect, cross-pressured. They have high regard for their work but feel that neither the college nor society gives them the recognition they deserve.

This group of cross-pressured voters, then, is the potential "swing vote"; these faculty members could vote either for or against collective bargaining. Which way they tend to vote in any given election depends on whether or not they receive the status and recognition they feel they deserve. And achieving these goals seems, in turn, to depend more and more on the resources that society is willing to devote to higher education. Given the increasing reluctance of society to spend additional money on any form of education, it seems likely that a growing number of college faculties will turn to collective bargaining.

effects of economic scarcity

Ideally, it might be useful to differentiate between economic and noneconomic issues at the bargaining table. But a neat distinction between the two would not be very helpful. In fact, as I argue elsewhere (Katz, 1973) the distinction may serve to conceal more than it reveals. What I mean to suggest, of course, is that issues apparently noneconomic have economic roots. For example, such contemporary issues as tenure, open admissions, independent study for students, and the current concern with teaching instead of research have an economic base that is often overlooked in the ongoing debate. Furthermore, economic stringency in higher education has raised these supposedly noneconomic concerns to new levels of urgency. Put simply, the current economic depression in higher education means that we can no longer afford the luxury of "slack politics."

Salary Issues. It is commonly believed that economic scarcity has had its greatest impact on salaries. At least at Temple, and presumbly at a number of other colleges and universities, this has not been the case. In 1972-1973, for example, the median salary at Temple was $14,500, which was just about average for the nation's colleges and universities as a whole. And at least at the lower three faculty ranks, average compensation at Temple was high enough to fall within the top 20 percent. Furthermore, the average salary increase at Temple for 1972-1973 was 6.3 percent, compared with a national average increase of only 5 percent.

But these rosy figures hardly dispose of salary as an issue. First, college professors, like other members of the middle class, are hurt by American tax policy. Temple faculty members pay a city wage tax, a state income tax, a state sales tax, high property taxes, and increasing social security taxes, as well as a federal income tax. For the average Temple faculty member, these taxes probably reduce his disposable income by 30 percent or more; as a result, he probably has available about $200 a week to maintain his status in society. In other words, even though Temple faculty members are not badly paid in comparison to faculty at other colleges and universities, their income is hardly commensurate with their own view of their status. Moreover, professional expectations regarding salary have continued to rise. Dramatic salary gains made by public school teachers and the very attractive salary schedule at the City University of New York have induced many faculty members to reevaluate their own salary expectations.

A second salary issue at Temple—and, I assume, at a number of other institutions as well—is that some institutional policies foster inequities. To name one, Temple's policy is to increase salaries by a percentage of the previous year's base salary. Thus, a 5 percent increase for a $20,000 employee ($1000) and a similar increase for a $10,000 employee ($500) actually widen the differential by $500. In fact, the actual situation is even worse. For 1972-1973, the average salary increase for a full professor was 6.2 percent, while instructors received only a 5.7 percent boost. Furthermore, the range of salaries within each rank appears to be extraordinarily large: the range for full professors was $15,500 to $31,000 in 1972-1973; for associate professors, $12,500 to $24,500; for assistant professors, $10,000 to $22,500; and for instructors, $8,000 to $14,000. While most faculty would accept the concept of merit pay, it is difficult to believe that differentials of this magnitude represent merit alone.

The easiest way to deal with these disparities is to introduce a salary schedule. This would serve to reduce the arbitrary nature of the current system. During the course of the election campaign at Temple, both the AFT and the FCBA proposed such schedules. The victory of the AAUP, which did not take a clear-cut position on the issue, could be interpreted to mean that the faculty had rejected the introduction of a salary schedule. However, it should be pointed out that Temple, like many other colleges and universities, goes to considerable lengths to maintain secrecy about individual salaries; accordingly, a faculty member cannot really compare his salary to that of his colleagues. In fact, the Petkov survey showed that most faculty members, asked to compare their salaries to those of their colleagues, indicated an inability to do so. Furthermore, the AAUP has now placed the highest priority on the development of a salary schedule and probably will make such a demand once actual negotiations begin.

But the mere acceptance of a salary schedule concept will not resolve the faculty's problem. If there is a limited amount of money available (say, 6 or 7 percent of the current salary budget), then in order to decrease the gap between high- and low-paid faculty, those at the lower end of the scale must be given substantial increases— and those at the top will have to settle for correspondingly small increases. But once a union accepts the premise that only a limited amount of money is available for salary increases, it puts itself in the highly undesirable position of having to reconcile opposing claims to that money. So, at least ideally, a union should attempt to increase the total size of the pie available.

This tactic, however, requires at least two resources that faculty unions often do not have. First, a union would need access to comprehensive budget information in order to have an effective voice in the overall allocation of the university's resources. (Unfortunately, the Pennsylvania Employee Relations Act limits the scope of collective bargaining and seems to reserve questions about the allocation of the total budget to "management.") Second, without a redistribution of internal resources, available money can come only from increased tuition or increased state funding. For a variety of reasons, increasing tuition would be neither desirable nor politic. And increased state appropriations would require a kind of political clout that less militant faculty unions, including the AAUP at Temple, do not seem capable of providing. Furthermore, as has happened at some other universities, the faculty union likely would end up negotiating with state officials rather than with the university administration, thereby inviting further external intrusions.

Tenure: A Central Issue. If the "relatively simple" salary issue raises difficult problems for the faculty union, the issue of job security poses virtually impossible ones. At Temple, as at many other state institutions whose enrollments mushroomed during the past decade, many of the young faculty members, hired during the late 1960s, are just now becoming eligible for tenure. Although exact figures are not available, probably at least 50 percent of Temple faculty were not tenured as of the fall of 1972. These 600 faculty members are coming up for tenure at a time when it has become quite difficult to achieve. Clearly, the issue of tenure has taken on a new importance for them, as borne out by the Petkov data: 32 percent of the tenured faculty as compared with 43 percent of the untenured faculty voted for the AFT in the run-off election. Furthermore, even the untenured faculty who voted for the AAUP ranked tenure among their highest priorities.

Several factors have combined to make tenure a salient issue at Temple. First, the nationwide surplus of Ph.D.s enables the university to release someone after six years and replace him with a young assistant professor or instructor at a considerably lower salary. Second, Temple appears to be caught in the squeeze between rising costs and decreasing enrollments. Consequently, the administration has announced a "job freeze" so that, in fact, there will be very few new hirings. For most departments, staff increases are barred, but a more flexible attitude exists toward replacements. Thus, in effect, the only way a new faculty member may be brought into a department is to deny tenure to an existing member of the faculty. Finally, as the recent study of tenure by the AAUP and the Association of American Colleges warns (*Faculty Tenure...*, 1973, pp. 49-50), many colleges are now in danger of becoming "tenured-in"; the study even goes so far as to recommend that no institution should allow more than one-half to two-thirds of its faculty to obtain tenure.

Given the confluence of these circumstances, it is reasonable to expect that the percentage of probationary faculty who receive tenure will decrease sharply. More important, for most faculty members the tenure decision will come to rest more on outside circumstances than on individual merit. The impact of this realization on the untenured faculty member is quite profound, for his future is determined more by impersonal market forces than by factors within his control; almost inevitably he has feelings of insecurity, frustration and alienation. It is not surprising, therefore, that the untenured faculty turn readily to collective bargaining in an attempt to regain control of their destinies.

Of course, many administrators and senior faculty members seem willing to allow the untenured faculty to bear the formidable costs of the current economic situation. They argue that an overly tenured faculty would stifle creativity, deny flexibility to college decision makers, and, in general, weaken the quality of the faculty. Furthermore, some senior faculty see the current situation as an opportunity to make selective judgments and thereby actually improve the quality of the faculty.

How to resolve this problem really depends on one's concept of tenure. According to the AAUP-AAC report (*Faculty Tenure...*, 1973) "tenure is viewed as a means of ensuring academic freedom and of providing sufficient economic security." And tenure means that "after the expiration of a probationary period, faculty members should have permanent or continuous tenure and that their service should be terminated only for adequate cause."

Further, "it is essential ... to understand the important distinction between *dismissal* and *nonreappointment*. . . . Dismissal is the termination of service during a tenure appointment. . . . Nonreappointment, by contrast, is the decision not to offer a further contract of employment, or not to award tenure." Within the meaning of the statement, dismissal can only follow a finding of adequate cause. Nonreappointment, however, is justified by any of the following: (1) unsatisfactory performance; (2) performance which is satisfactory but incompatible with the institution's "educational objectives and standards"; (3) full staffing at the tenure level; (4)

changes in the institution's academic program; and (5) budgetary constraints. The Commission also points out that the preceding list is not inclusive; other reasons would be satisfactory so long as they did not violate academic freedom or constitutional rights or were not arbitrary or capricious. From the foregoing it is clear: probationary faculty members enjoy no "right" to tenure, and a university may properly deny someone tenure regardless of his professional qualifications.

The justification for this position is twofold: first, tenure exists principally to protect academic freedom (and not simply job security); second, receiving tenure signifies admittance into the academic guild and is therefore significantly different from the job security and seniority provisions often associated with labor contracts in industry. In most labor contracts, one is entitled to "continuous employment" unless he is demonstrably incompetent. Accordingly, the employee does enjoy something closely akin to a "right of tenure." This latter pattern is often followed in the public schools and in many two-year colleges. While these pages are not the place to argue the merits of either position, if the traditional university model is followed and the economic depression in higher education continues, we must be prepared to deal with large numbers of faculty members who will never achieve tenure.

Senior Faculty Stakes. Finally, economic scarcity in higher education has had an impact on tenured senior faculty as well. Much of the freedom traditionally associated with academic life is actually a product of plentiful resources. Academic institutions are notoriously poorly managed. As a result, faculty members often have been allowed to make many important decisions about what to teach, when to schedule classes, how much energy to devote to research, summer employment, and class size, among others. During the carefree days of the 1960s, it made little difference to university administrators how faculty members decided these questions since available resources were adequate to support a variety of programs.

However, legislatures and state departments of education have become keenly interested in how faculty members spend their time. In Pennsylvania, for instance, the state legislature recently considered a bill which would have required twelve-hour teaching loads for all faculty members in state colleges. Although the bill was not acted on by the state senate, it no doubt indicates much closer public scrutiny and state control. Moreover, all faculty members have been required to submit "productivity reports," and the university is being asked to justify individual faculty positions in terms of the number of credit hours generated. In addition, Pennsylvania's State Commissioner of Education (a former professor of political science himself) has taken steps to evaluate the duplication of programs among the state's colleges and universities.

While college professors might not be inclined to take these challenges seriously, there is evidence that the state's attitudes are shared in some measure by college administrators. At Temple, for example, university administrators have made it clear that they felt managerial control slipped from their grasp during the fat sixties and that current budget crises provide opportunities to reassert that control.

In summary, two points concerning the influence of the economy must be emphasized. First, higher education is in a state of economic depression that has adversely affected all colleges and universities in one way or another. Unfortunately, this phenomenon does not seem to be temporary. Even with a more progressive administration in Washington and with uniformly enlightened state governments, the economic crisis will be difficult to resolve. What would help? A progressive system of taxation, major cutbacks in military spending, and greater social control over the allocation of resources all could serve to make more money available to education. But, regrettably, there is little likelihood that these changes will occur.

A second point arises out of the possibility that colleges and universities could make more efficient use of the limited resources they command. Given the realities of current American politics, this second alternative will probably be the one selected. The crucial question here is who controls the allocation of resources within colleges and universities. This control is the key.

Thus, how the faculty will emerge from the current economic crises will depend on both their willingness to seek aggressively a greater share of the nation's economic resources and their ability to influence the internal distribution of the limited resources available to their particular institutions. It is to these two issues that the remainder of this paper is directed.

governance and power

The current model for the distribution of authority within colleges and universities is commonly referred to as shared governance. According to this model, the faculty has primary responsibility for decision making in such professional areas as tenure, dismissal, curriculum, grades, and both the content and method of instruction. But, of course, an enormous gulf separates "primary responsibility" and "final authority." The model recognizes that final authority in all areas rests with governing boards, although their power is tempered both by tradition and by the need to give reasoned explanations for denials of faculty recommendations.

The shared governance model is derived from medieval constitutionalism. According to Wilson C. McWilliams (1972, p. 16), medieval constitutionalism made it "the duty of a king to consult with representatives of his subjects," and "rulers were morally obliged to give reasons to the ruled and to hear counter-arguments." The subjects were morally obliged to obey the ruler, provided he could make "rationally compelling arguments" for his position. Of course, the subjects of a medieval king always had an option not available to contemporary faculty members—they, at least, had the power to overthrow the king and install a new one. The Industrial Revolution swept away the medieval system, and "subjects" were replaced by "citizens" who enjoyed legally enforceable rights. American faculty members, however, still seem to inhabit a medieval world—as subjects—and their own "revolution" may not be too far away.

Faculty Influence and Responsibility. It might be argued that whatever the logical shortcomings of the shared governance concept, in many places the will of the faculty is respected and they often do play significant roles in policy making. No doubt this is true. But in order to reach a reasoned evaluation of shared governance, one must consider the faculty's spheres of influence in relation to the real curbs on its power.

The faculty has exercised great responsibility in at least three areas. At most good universities, individual faculty members control what they teach and how they teach it; in other words, academic freedom is respected. Also, acting through its governing mechanism, the faculty determines academic degree requirements. And at many institutions, the faculty plays a determining role in personnel matters: hiring, tenure, and dismissal.

But the faculty's freedom to make decisions in these areas depends on broader university policies that are formulated with little or no faculty consultation. To illustrate: the overall university budget, and the allocations made within that budget, determine the limited framework within which the faculty can operate. For example, whether Professor X teaches a seminar with twenty students or an introductory course with two hundred students is determined not only by his skills and preferences but by the university's capacity to allow small, uneconomical courses. Or, whether Professor Y obtains tenure depends both on his colleagues' evaluation of him and on the university's willingness to see more professors receive tenure.

These basic constraints did not serve to limit seriously the faculty's freedom during the 1960s, but clearly they have a substantial impact today. At many universities, the faculty has come to accept this system of constraints and tends to make decisions that will be acceptable to the university administration, operating under what Richard Neustadt has called the law of "anticipated reaction." At other universities, the faculty may ignore these restrictions, but only at the risk of confronting the administration. In these situations, the faculty quite likely will learn the hard way the difference between "primary responsibility" and "final authority."

Bargaining: An Erosion of Faculty Power? During the course of the campaign at Temple, a large segment of the faculty expressed concern that collective bargaining would result in a loss of control over tenure and promotion decisions—an issue that extends far beyond Temple's campus. By and large, Temple's faculty felt they had been successful in gaining administrative approval for their personnel recommendations. They feared that collective bargaining, especially the introduction of arbitration, would threaten their influence. To some of the Temple faculty, the issue is not that the administration will deny tenure to individuals recommended by the faculty; rather, the fear is that an outside arbitrator will grant tenure to someone whom neither the faculty nor the administration supports. Trying to limit an arbitrator's authority to procedural irregularities would not, they say, be sufficient protection, for efforts to distinguish between procedure and substance simply do not succeed (see Finkin, 1973, pp. 66-86). Moreover, the AAUP at Temple is not impressed by the argument that impartial arbitration is necessary to safeguard against a department's acting capriciously against an unpopular probationary faculty member. Most good universities, they submit, have some sort of campuswide faculty personnel committee to which an aggrieved faculty member may appeal. At Temple, for example, the Faculty Senate Personnel Committee has recommended tenure for some individuals who had not been recommended by their own departments. This sort of procedure, they argue, provides an adequate safeguard against arbitrary departmental action.

These are impressive arguments, but for at least two reasons they are not persuasive. First, the situation that the AAUP and others fear is probably the exception; there is no reason to assume that every faculty member who is denied tenure will seek arbitration. Indeed, relatively few faculty members who are denied tenure at Temple even bother to use the available internal appeal mechanisms. Second, and more important, I believe that the possibility of arbitration will force departmental and college personnel committees to take their jobs more seriously. I am acquainted with few personnel decisions that were based on serious consideration of teaching ability, critical appraisal of scholarly work, or thought about the long-term needs of the department. Rather, tenure decisions too often are based on rumor, quantity of publication, and whether or not the candidate has offended anyone. While it may be impossible to state the criteria for tenure with great precision, professional responsibility requires us to create mechanisms by which a candidate's performance can be fairly judged. Frankly, the availability of arbitration may be just the force that compels the faculty to take its professional responsibilities more seriously.

Many faculty members and administrators at Temple fear that collective bargaining will create new bureaucracies and rigidities. They are apprehensive that the open and flexible nature of the university will be jeopardized. But the threat of bureaucracy and rigidity stems not from collective bargaining; rather, the threat is posed by the desire of state officials and university administrators to assert greater managerial control because the current economic situation requires greater accountability and rationality in the allocation of resources.

Thus, collective bargaining must be viewed basically as a protective, defensive, and in some ways conservative reaction by faculty to sweeping changes in the nature of academic life. In this context, the "legalisms" feared by some faculty are really attributable to the already changed nature of the university. Collective bargaining, with its emphasis on contractual rights, simply marks the passing of more traditional relationships that prevailed in easier times. Viewed in this light, the causes of faculty discontent fall beyond the control of individual academic institutions. Ultimately, faculty discontent grows out of economic and political changes over which the university itself has little influence. But faculty members must not lose sight of the corollary lesson: despite the external origins of the problems confronting them, resort to internal, collective organization is essential to defend their legitimate interests.

politics

The early advocates of collective bargaining at Temple had two important political motivations. In the first place, they sought to replace the existing system of power with a more democratic one in which faculty members would recognize their common interests and promote those interests through collective bargaining. Second, they hoped the faculty would come to recognize that its future depends on external factors and would unite with other liberal and progressive social forces to promote their joint interests. Although only a very small percentage of the faculty had thought these matters through at the beginning, a larger number of faculty members probably shared these motivations in one way or another.

Some faculty members at Temple, especially the founders of the FCBA, express concern about the growth of the administrative staff at Temple and are afraid that the faculty is losing its traditional control over academic matters. For them, collective bargaining is an attempt to reassert and maintain that faculty role. In truth, they are not enthusiastic about collective bargaining and would prefer to view it as a back-up to more traditional mechanisms such as the faculty senate. Others, the AFT partisans at Temple, would prefer to see collective bargaining replace traditional governance mechanisms.

But both of these groups, at least in the short run, are in for disappointment. The Pennsylvania Employee Relations Act limits collective bargaining to wages, fringe benefits, and working conditions. The law carefully exempts "managerial rights," which are to be considered only in "meet and discuss" sessions. Furthermore, the Pennsylvania Supreme Court has narrowly construed the meaning of "working conditions" in a public school case and probably would not take a different position in a college or university case. Consequently, in the current battle over control of the university, the administration will clearly have the advantage over those who wish to use bargaining to reassert traditional faculty influence.

Those who would prefer to see control in the hands of "workers' councils" will likely be even more frustrated. State law, and the collective bargaining relationship itself, will probably serve to separate even further faculty from administration, and bargaining will focus more and more on the employee-employer relationship. Thus, any notion that collective bargaining can be used by the faculty to seize control of the university is, I am afraid, a chimera.

Faculty as Employees. However, in the longer run, the development of an employee orientation among faculty members will have important and perhaps beneficial consequences. In the first place, such a development would speed the affiliation of faculty members with organized labor. The AFT, of course, is already affiliated with the AFL-CIO, and strong pressures within the NEA will probably force it to develop alliances with at least some elements of organized labor. Even the AAUP likely will be forced to seek its own accommodation with the labor movement. At the same time, other professional and white-collar workers are slowly coming into the trade union movement.

If these trends continue, an emerging coalition of public school teachers, college professors, and other social service workers quite likely will constitute the largest single group within organized labor. Moreover, some evidence indicates that unions of this sort are politically more sophisticated and radical than are some of the more traditional craft unions. And in a larger sense, the continuing unionization of professional workers is bound to have an important impact on the internal politics of the labor movement and, ultimately, on the politics of the nation.

What About Students? Another consideration is the stake students have in faculty unionism. It is sometimes claimed that if faculty members think of themselves as employees, then students necessarily will suffer. This is an issue that troubles many faculty members and administrators. If I understand the argument correctly, the allegation is that if faculty members think of themselves as employees, they will take less of a personal interest in their students; they will be "clock watchers," and to protect their own interests they will oppose student involvement in university decision making. But we should recall that these same charges were leveled against faculty before the advent of collective bargaining. Although it may be true that collective bargaining will bring faculty-student conflict to the surface, that is quite different from claiming that collective bargaining is a major cause of such conflict.

There is, of course, the danger that faculty unions will follow the model of the American Medical Association, which, it is sometimes alleged, pursues its own interests at the expense of society.

While it is doubtful that a faculty union could ever achieve the power or status of the AMA, the problem of accountability still arises. In a legal sense, faculty members will continue to be accountable to the administration. But in a broader sense, means must be developed to assure a sense of social responsibility. Faculty unionism, *within the context of organized labor,* may actually be the mechanism to promote this sort of responsibility. Just as the participation of professional workers in the labor movement could revitalize the movement, so would that participation modify and shape the demands of the professional workers. If, for example, the faculty of a state university were to solicit the aid of organized labor in obtaining increased state funding, then it seems likely that labor, in turn, could make certain demands of the faculty. Obviously the actual process would be more subtle than this. The important point is that unionization can provide the framework in which faculty and labor can influence and provide support for each other.

In summary, it is imperative for us to view faculty unionization with the broadest possible perspective and in terms of its long-range effects. American colleges and universities have never been ivory towers; they are part of the total social system and both affect and are profoundly affected by the economic and political dynamics of society. Faculty unionism must be seen as a response to these broad influences and, in my view, can be properly evaluated only in terms of its likely impact on those dynamics.

references

Finkin, M. W. "Grievance Procedures." In E. D. Duryea, R. S. Fisk, and Associates. *Faculty Unions and Collective Bargaining.* San Francisco: Jossey-Bass, 1973.

Katz, E. "Political Opposition in America." In B. McClennan (Ed.), *Political Opposition and Dissent.* New York: Dernellen, 1973.

McWilliams, W. C. "The American Constitutions." In G. M. Pomper and others, *The Performance of American Government.* New York: Free Press, 1972.

Metzger, W. P. "Academic Tenure in America: A Historical Essay." In *Faculty Tenure: A Report and Recommendations by the Commission on Academic Tenure in Higher Education.* San Francisco: Jossey-Bass, 1973.

Ellis Katz is an associate professor of political science and the foundations of education at Temple University, where he has directed the General Education Program for Teachers and served as co-chairman of AFT Local 2253.

*If properly understood, collective bargaining
can strengthen management's effectiveness
in the decision-making process.*

collective bargaining: opportunities for "management"

caesar j. naples

As if the disaffection with institutions of higher education expressed by students, alumni, the public, and state legislators were
not enough to burden college administrators, many faculties
throughout the country have chosen to require that administrators
now respond in a mode vastly different from their traditional one.
For a variety of reasons, faculty collective bargaining has dramatically changed the role of numerous university administrators, has
affected the way they analyze problems, and has even fostered the
development of a new breed.

Why college faculties are rapidly divesting themselves of roles
and relationships which have survived eight hundred years of
plagues, depressions, and wars is adequately documented in this
volume and elsewhere. For purposes of this commentary, I believe
it is sufficient to point out that a significant part of their motiva-
tion may lie in an increasingly popular faculty perception: unless
faculty members reassert themselves and firmly establish their authority through collectively negotiated agreements, bolstered by the
force of the law, other powerful claimants may effectively proscribe

the traditional faculty role in helping to determine institutional policy and direction.

Because of this new phenomenon, administrators are confronted with a dilemma: whether to adapt to faculty collective bargaining—and perhaps further encourage its development—or whether to resist what may well be inevitable in an effort to preserve as much as possible of existing "collegial" relationships. I believe there is not much doubt about the direction in which faculties will move: they will gravitate toward bargaining. Administrators, finding themselves beset from all sides to change the ways institutions of higher education are conducted, *must* adapt, and such adaptation will further drive faculties to consider collective bargaining as an alternative to traditional governance processes.

My thesis is perhaps an unusual one. Contrary to the fears and anxieties of many college administrators, I conclude that the process of adapting to collective bargaining can actually strengthen the role of management in higher education, and in some very important ways.

the conditioning of administrators

College administrators are not particularly comfortable with the label "manager," and I suspect that its use finds acceptance only because of the employee-relations backdrop of collective bargaining and because other terms have not readily been created. This is not to say that we in academe enjoy indulging in self-delusion. Rather, our resistance to being branded "management" is a product of centuries of conditioning. Traditionally, faculties have emphasized the fact that the role of administrator is just what the name implies: custodian, expeditor, caretaker of that collection of resources needed to support and sustain the process of education which takes place in classrooms and laboratories. Faculties felt that they themselves should develop institutional policies, and the function of administrators was to carry out the direction received from senates, committees, and other deliberative faculty bodies.

Not surprisingly, administrators' terms and conditions of employment reflected this secondary role in which they were cast. After all, the salaries and fringe benefits received by most career administrators were ordinarily inferior to those of teaching faculty, and, most dramatically, job security for administrators was nonexistent. And while the lowliest instructor was guaranteed by

AAUP standards nine months to a year's time to seek other employment, most administrators could be released with no notice at all.

Many senior administrators came from the ranks of faculty or their selection was heavily influenced by faculty search committees. The activities of many more administrators are still monitored by faculty committees created specifically for that purpose according to the campus's articles of governance. That method of selection tends to perpetuate the traditional view of the proper, ancillary role of administration.

It is interesting to note, in reviewing the traits characterizing traditional top-level administrators, that a premium seems to have been placed on identity with faculty: possession of the terminal degree, experience at all levels of faculty life, and an eschewing of a systems or business approach to administration. To compare, exchange, or reveal to another institution information on salaries, work load data, faculty-student ratios, and the like was somehow regarded as violation of privacy, and this institutionalized custom acted as an effective check on the usefulness of these management techniques. Consequently, the resultant measure of an administrator's effectiveness (underscored by the absence of an outside basis for comparison) was, at bottom, how much he behaved like a faculty member and how well he was regarded by the faculty.

the old order changeth

The first pressure for change came from "outside the family": from legislators and government agencies and from the public—all of whom required a responsiveness and an accountability from college administrators heretofore unknown. In addition, students demanded relevant programs and a rearrangement of priorities that would allocate resources to meet their felt needs. At the same time, alumni contributions flagged and government support slackened, in part because of the perceived anarchy pervading the campuses. Members of the general public demanded—and, indeed, continue to demand—that colleges and universities respond to current social problems in order to justify the enormous investments involved. These various groups demanded that administrators change the direction of their institutions according to a schedule that did not always permit the collegial deliberation and careful base-touching characteristic of the traditional governance mechanisms. The message was clear: get things done now or get out. Many administrators, I am sure, chose the latter path and were replaced by others, who, teaming with those who remained, accepted or even welcomed the changed role.

Eight hundred years of tradition were not without their lessons, and by the end of the decade many faculties perceived that numerous important decisions were being made outside the internal governance structures. While faculty pressures undoubtedly resulted in some resignations or terminations of administrators who failed to consult, many administrators, when measured by their governing boards against the new standards of how well they satisfied those outside pressures, survived and even flourished. I surmise that it is at this point that collective bargaining begins to take its place alongside traditional governance as an appropriate approach to resolving the needs of faculties to regain their authority.

why bargaining

If traditional governance works at all, it is because: (a) there is a readily identifiable commonality of purpose among participants in the governance process; (b) there is at least the appearance of participation satisfying to most; and (c) there is loyalty to the process which tends to cause participants to be loyal to the decisions reached (peer pressure tends to keep dissidents in line).

So long as an important measure of an administrator's performance was his ability to please the faculty, traditional governance best suited that end, since decisions reached thereby are generally acceptable. (I suspect that decisions may be substantively acceptable merely because of the process utilized in reaching them.)

It should be clear, however, that once that standard is changed, the ultimate effectiveness of traditional governance, from the manager's point of view, is lessened. Nevertheless, faculty ire is not normally sought after by any but the most foolhardy, and if existing processes no longer meet the needs of each participant, other methods must be devised to render acceptable necessary institutional decisions. Further, many believe that a diminution of faculty authority is detrimental to institutional health and that some method, preferably reinforced by the force of law, must be found to protect that threatened authority from outside assailants. Collective bargaining may now be viewed as a device designed to accomplish those ends.

A collective bargaining contract is recognized by all but the most revolutionary as practically inviolate. It can serve as an almost impenetrable barrier to legislators seeking to increase work loads, to the public seeking to remove professors with unpopular beliefs, to students seeking involvement in decision making, and to alumni seeking still other changes. It enables the manager to affirm his respect for the faculty's right to participate in decisions while, if he is skillful, he can retain the freedom of action necessary to carry out his managerial responsibilities. Under collective bargaining, a manager may evidence this respect by recognizing the union, by bargaining in good faith through long and arduous sessions, and by signing an agreement. As is discussed below in a different context, he can, in the agreement, limit faculty authority in many areas—and thereby preserve for himself the flexibility to act in areas falling outside the contractual boundaries.

Once an agreement is consummated, it becomes the union's burden to seek faculty concurrence, while the manager is able to turn away inquiries about the adequacy of contractual provisions by pointing out that the faculty's own union agreed. Furthermore, after experiencing the criticism, rhetoric and angry diatribes which so often characterize collective bargaining, governing boards may view faculty complaints about an administrator's toughminded "un-responsiveness" as solid testimony to his effectiveness as a management advocate.

Collective bargaining, viewed as a process, fares well when compared to traditional governance mechanisms:

(a) The act of sitting at the bargaining table, patiently exploring, explaining, making offers and counteroffers, striving to reach agreement may be read by each participant as acceptance by the other of his right to be involved.

(b) The ritual evidence of the process—public meetings when demands are delivered; periodic bulletins reporting progress, no progress, or, most engaging, "no comment" (implying hard bargaining is being conducted behind those closed doors)—is generally enough to convince most observers that participation in decision making is taking place. Additionally, most collective bargaining agreements create other avenues of dialogue such as monthly labor-management meetings to discuss current issues, and the right to grieve—often to a binding conclusion and to an outside impartial arbitrator—which may actually improve faculty participation.

(c) The faculty union seeks loyalty to the process by exerting peer pressures, by vigorously supporting faculty grievances, and the like. Failure to support the union—and abide by the negotiated contract—tends to undermine the union and weaken its hand vis-a-vis management.

Collective bargaining, therefore, tends to meet the needs of both participants who, in days gone by, may have been satisfied by traditional governance processes but in different ways. Furthermore, with universities being subjected to new pressures of great intensity, the role of management and the needs of the faculty have both changed. In sum, collective bargaining appears to meet the requirements, resulting from altered roles, of both administrators and faculty.

dividends for management

In traditional governance operations, the administration tends not to be involved in developing a faculty position. Issues are proposed and discussed among faculty members, and a position is developed which then is presented to the administration for concurrence. Resistance or an attempt to modify or compromise is often viewed by the faculty as an insult to their ability to deliberate responsibly. The underlying assumption seems to be that the faculty is perfectly capable of determining institution policies with little need for administrative involvement.

But the heart of collective bargaining is compromise. Collective bargaining presumes that two parties are involved: labor and management. Each is assumed to have its proper point of view and the authority to speak for and to commit its constituents. A union demands to negotiate with a management fully empowered to make commitments and to reach an agreement; so the process implicitly cedes to management the right to say "yes" or "no." What has happened, then, is a quite profound change: faculties have accepted management's right to manage (rather than merely administer) the institution. Of course, the union's emphasis is upon winning substantive concessions from management and not upon the implicit change in management's role. But the horse-trading that takes place merely serves to reinforce management's claim to authority.

Also, since the process is recognized as one of compromise, management has the opportunity to affect the faculty position through debate and persuasion in a context where the parties expect a dialogue. It is a process of advocacy and debate rather than merely expected concurrence.

The manager must be able to respond at the bargaining table.

This ability is enhanced by having at the table spokesmen for those interests affected by bargaining. A bargaining team may, for example, consist of a business or finance person, another who is involved in personnel matters, and one who can speak for the academic policy makers, in addition to the primary negotiator.

To respond, managers need data to document their positions and to analyze and meet those of the union. One of bargaining's most beneficial side effects on university management is improvement, resulting from necessity, in the collection, storage, retrieval, accuracy, and relevance of data concerning the institution, its policies and practices.

A further side effect is the establishment or improvement of existing channels of communications and exchange of data with sister institutions. Historically, institutions of higher education were reluctant to exchange any but the most basic information. Unions, apparently, have little respect for such insularity and are constantly presenting as models the salary schedules, benefit programs, work load data, and other institutional vital statistics from comparable colleges and universities in an effort to convince management. The only way for management to verify these assertions is through checking with managers at the other institutions. Further, in developing its positions in response to union demands, management will find it helpful to make its own comparisons of the salaries, fringes, policies, and practices at peer institutions. That collective bargaining will have a leveling effect on such crucial matters is obvious.

The manager will also need to develop sources of information regarding practices within his own institution. For example, an administrator can become familiar with the practices and procedures involved in peer review in tenure decisions on his own campus in a relatively short time.*

The process of collective bargaining generally has been feared by college managers, who terrify their colleagues with stories of how such-and-such a university was forced to its knees by hard faculty bargaining or was required to expend huge sums of money as a result of an arbitrator's interpretation of a poorly drafted contract clause. While such stories undoubtedly have some basis in fact,

*Obtaining these data in a multicampus system such as SUNY becomes a bit more challenging. And attempting to reach conclusions about whether any one practice is better than any other—and should, therefore, become the contractual standard imposed upon other departments, schools or campuses, —can be mind-jarring.

most significant adverse effects can be avoided by an understanding of the collective bargaining process, by adequate preparation for it, and through appropriate skill and care in drafting contract language. In fact, collective bargaining presents management with important opportunities to improve its position in the decision-making process.

bargaining process facilitates agreement

Traditional governance tends to function on an issue-by-issue basis. In this situation faculty attention and energy (and pressure) can be focused on a particular problem with great intensity. The dialogue is generally public, facilitating faculty mobilization. Tempers cool down only when the specific issue is resolved satisfactorily but are ready to erupt again the next week when a new issue catches the spotlight. When so much attention is concentrated on the participants, it is difficult to compromise without engendering severe constituent criticism.

Collective bargaining, on the other hand, presents dozens of issues for resolution at the same time. As the parties bargain, a concession in one area can serve as the quid pro quo for a modification of position in another. In this way, agreement can be reached on a comprehensive collection of issues, an agreement which might be difficult, if not impossible, in the prebargaining forum. Because of these trade-offs, each party may achieve substantive advances in areas beyond reach if one issue alone were the subject of discussions. Of course, the success of such "horse-trading" depends on the participants having different priorities in relation to each particular issue, but such differences merely make the bargaining sessions more interesting.

The fact that most collective bargaining takes place in private sessions rather than in meetings open to the general public also tends to facilitate agreement. While participants would be foolhardy if they did not consult carefully with their constituents by means of some kind of policy committee selected to represent the spectrum of their interests, private sessions tend to encourage open communication and compromise.

Modification of one's position can be accomplished without having to justify or reveal a general strategy. Inordinate pressure from "one-issue" constituent subgroups is minimized. Negotiating in a fishbowl, by contrast, tends to result in playing to one's audience rather than in meaningful communications between the parties. Finally, most administrative agencies enforcing the obligation to bargain in good faith tend to frown on public bargaining sessions as unnecessarily interfering with a party's ability to develop its position sequentially with respect to any particular issue.

stability of the contract

Because of the multitude of issues on which agreement is reached in a contract and because trade-offs have woven them together, collective bargaining agreements frequently have lengthy terms, often up to three years. If management agrees to abide by a particular procedure for the term of the contract, it will be so bound for that time. Similarly, if a faculty union agrees, for example, that in cases of nonreappointment no reason need be given by the president, neither it nor any faculty member covered by the agreement can successfully require a change in that policy during its term.

Traditional governance arrangements, on the other hand, fundamentally rely on the continuing respect each participant has for the other's contributions. If the faculty feels that a particular campus policy has outlived its usefulness, it often can have the rules changed in mid-semester.

From management's point of view, the stability inherent in a collective bargaining agreement is significant. While management's obligations are fixed for a period of time by the provisions of an agreement, its opportunities for freedom of action (which may be defined either by specific reference in a carefully drafted document or by implication) are also preserved. Such stability, amid higher education's world of accelerating change, can be a significant benefit to management.

administering the agreement

Administration of the collective bargaining agreement is every bit as important as the negotiations. Hard-won commitments, carefully delineated by precise language during bargaining, may be lost through poor contract administration. Each manager must understand the contract and as much of the bargaining history as he can absorb. In a collective bargaining context, as in most others, a manager must be confident of his proper sphere of activity. Not only must he be aware of what the contract says he *must* do or refrain from doing, he must understand what he *may* do without running afoul of the contract's provisions or the union's right to become involved in his decisions. Probably as much managerial flexibility has been lost because managers feared that a potential decision might be challenged by a union as has been lost through concessions actually made at the bargaining table.

Given the pluralistic nature of most faculties and the wariness with which they have approached collective bargaining even at those campuses which have opted for it, managers will find it necessary to consult with faculty subgroups, such as senates, which are not integral parts of the faculty union. The union, in seeking contractual protection of its hard-won bargaining rights, often demands that management restrict its discussions with faculty representatives to the union.

Though this union posture is understandable, management's obligation is to restrict to the union only negotiations over terms and conditions of employment, as provided by the scope of the bargaining obligation. At the bargaining table, management should insist on contractual language so limited as to leave itself free to conduct discussions with other appropriate faculty interest groups, as the need arises. Such a provision is not intended to undermine the union's exclusive representation status, and management's contractual prerogatives should, in practice, be exercised with suitable caution. Discussions with a rival union, for example, are generally unwise. Additionally, issues which could properly fall within the gamut of negotiable terms and conditions of employment should be taken up with the union, not with the senate.

the scope of bargaining: some mistaken assumptions

At least at first glance, one might suppose that managers' lives would be a lot simpler if federal or state bargaining statutes clearly delineated the negotiable issues. But the better statutes do not. Regardless of the length of any such list, unions are certain to raise other issues over which it would be in the best interests of both parties to negotiate. Thus, contrary to what many university administrators might expect, a prior restriction in the statute which limits the scope of bargaining will prove to be unhelpful.

Why is this so? Although a weak union may be put off by such a restriction, in a situation with a disparity of power, management is likely to be able to restrict the scope anyway. When the union is strong, experience shows that it probably will be able to work its will irrespective of the law. Indeed, in the latter case, management will have difficulty in securing a contract unless it agrees to make concessions in the prohibited areas. Finally, there will always be cases in which, for one reason or another, management—rather than the union—wants to include a contract provision covering an excluded subject. (I think, for example, of a clause to protect a particular policy or practice from outside assault.) So, over the long haul, surprising as it may seem, nobody really benefits from such a restriction.

It is clear, though, that if the parties have chosen to include a particular matter in their agreement, arbitrators and administrative agencies will find that such a topic falls within the scope of bargaining. Thus, management's discussion of this issue with another group likely will be considered an unfair labor practice in violation of the union's exclusive bargaining rights. Consequently, it is imperative that managers consider carefully each issue before agreeing to include it in a contract.

An example may serve to illuminate. A faculty union may demand that management include a clause in the agreement that the faculty senate shall continue to exist and that its committees shall continue their roles. Though such a provision might seem innocuous enough, its teeth will be revealed during the next round of bargaining. At this time, the union may demand that the senate be severely modified or perhaps abolished. (No union enjoys the ominous presence of a potential competitor for faculty support thriving in its own backyard, and, not surprisingly, many unions view senates in just this way.) Management may have forfeited its right, by its prior, innocent agreement, to argue that governance matters fall outside the scope of bargaining.

the fate of traditional structures

I have dwelled at some length on the theme that faculty collective bargaining is not the *bete noir* it is so often assumed to be by university administrators and that, moreover, the collective bargaining process affords management a number of important opportunities. To be sure, it is almost always better for management to bargain with a strong union rather than a weak one; management would rather know that the union can "deliver" once it reaches agreement at the table. But managers—and faculties—should consider long and hard before abandoning traditional governance structures in favor of collective bargaining.

In the first place, higher education has not yet had enough experience with bargaining to justify writing obituaries for faculty senates. We do not know, for example, what effect collective bargaining—with its tendency to polarize faculties and administration into adversary roles—will have on the process of peer selection and evaluation. Most private sector unions willingly cede to management the right to hire, promote, and take disciplinary action against employees. The traditional involvement of faculties in these processes may well be lost if adversary collective bargaining is substituted for the more collegial traditional relationships. To date, administrative agencies charged with the authority to define the mandatory scope of negotiable issues, and arbitrators who will interpret agreements, have not yet decided a sufficient variety of cases to enable management or unions to discern their proper scope of activity. When this is done we will all learn whether private sector principles apply to higher education.

It may very well be in the interests of both the union and management to continue to support the existence of a faculty senate to serve as sort of a "neutral ground" in which issues too volatile or disruptive to handle at the bargaining table may be worked out. This "no-man's land" can be especially valuable in the early stages of a bargaining relationship when the union is still seeking to win the confidence of the faculty and the respect of management.

I maintain that such a drastic step as abolishing faculty senates is entirely premature at this stage of development. For if traditional governance is destined to wither away, its fate will become apparent soon enough. When the union feels that management is able to circumvent it by dealing with the senate over issues for which the union has firm faculty support, the union will be in a position to mount an effective bargaining-table attack on collegial governance. Conversely, when management perceives the senate as a vehicle through which the union may achieve advances it was unable to secure at the bargaining table, I believe the time for collegial governance will be past. In the meantime, however, both parties still have much to gain from the senate's continued existence.

Written contracts and binding arbitration are not the threat to managerial authority feared by many. Rather, collective bargaining presents management with the opportunity to delineate areas of managerial freedom of action which were cloudy and unclear under traditional governance. The negotiation and administration of contracts will tend to require that managers develop resources and skills essential to effective management. Yet traditional faculty governance mechanisms add significantly to the process of decision making and should continue to exist, at least for the time being.

Collective bargaining has settled like a mist upon the campus, clouding and obscuring traditional roles and relationships. Management's challenge is to look through the mist, to perceive the opportunities offered by collective bargaining, to understand them—and to seize upon them.

Caesar J. Naples is assistant vice chancellor of the State University of New York, serving as the University's chief employee relations officer for negotiations, contract administration, and grievance processing. A graduate of Yale and SUNY Buffalo Law School, in private practice he represented teachers, librarians, police and firefighters unions in the public sector, as well as management in the private sector. In government service Mr. Naples served as counsel and staff director to New York State's Select Joint Legislative Committee on Public Employment Relations and, subsequently, on Governor Nelson Rockefeller's staff as assistant director of employee relations.

*Faculty members have special responsibilities
to assess the implications of faculty collective
bargaining for academic governance and
assure exemplary academic self government
as a model for other social institutions.*

academic bargaining: power changes for everyone?

robert k. carr

Collective bargaining by faculty members very often will result in
substantial changes in an institution's governance system; the role
and authority of everyone—trustees, administrators, faculty members, and students, as well as persons and agencies off campus—will
be altered. Some will gain in power and responsibility, others lose.
My findings and observations on faculty bargaining, based on more
than two years of research with Daniel K. VanEyck between mid-
1970 and early 1973, are set forth at some length in *Faculty Bargaining Comes to the Campus,* published in 1973 by the American
Council on Education. In the present paper, however, I shall limit
my comments to several salient issues that are, to my way of think-
ing, cause for considerable concern.

two roles for faculty

Faculty members can play at least two quite different roles
in the further development of faculty collective bargaining. Some—

as specialists in, say, politics, law, economics, education, and business administration—can and should help the faculties of which they are members decide whether in their particular institutional contexts they want to turn to collective bargaining, and, if they do, which of several available models best suits local needs. It is also reasonable to suppose that where faculty bargaining is already taking place, such specialists should be active participants. Academicians must recognize that collective bargaining is a continuous process. Living under a contract may well require at least as much attention and effort as does its negotiation. Thus, these specialists should expect to serve not only as members of the teams that negotiate contracts, but as officers of faculty unions and as members of the many agencies that may be required to administer the terms of a contract. We may call this the activist role.

A second role for faculty members is the opportunity and responsibility to use their special competences to observe, evaluate, and report on faculty bargaining as an aspect of university governance and politics. How is the process working on particular campuses and in American higher education in general? What models are taking shape; where, and why, and with what results? What is the impact of faculty bargaining on existing patterns of university governance—or nongovernance? We may call this the scholarly role.

The first role can often be highly personal and partisan. Scholars should use their expertise and influence in well-conceived efforts to persuade their faculty colleagues to adopt and follow policies that will best serve their common interests and needs—both as employees of their institutions and as the professional people who, more than any other members of an academic community, run the institution. The second role must necessarily be, in large measure, dispassionate and even-handed. Facts must be reported as fully and as accurately as possible; conclusions must be as sound and impersonal as a scholar can make them.

That in playing these two roles faculty members may find themselves coping with troublesome conflicts of interest needs no stressing, for this conflict is well known to scholars who have become activists in community politics or even in the governance of their own academic institutions. At their best, faculty have managed to keep their activist and scholarly interests, needs, and achievements reasonably distinct, yet compatible. In the main, the record is one in which the academic profession can take pride. Let us hope that the same will be true of the dual responsibility of faculty people with respect to the problems posed by collective bargaining.

bargaining and institutional governance

Faculty bargaining is most usefully and properly viewed as part of the evolution of university governance; it is an option or model that must and will be carefully considered in this era in which change in the structuring and operation of colleges and universities is probably more rapid and far-reaching than at any time in the last three and a half centuries. There are those, I know, who argue that faculty bargaining can be confined to the economic realm, as in the traditional industry model of employer-employee relations, while by other means the faculty continues to play an appropriate role in the creation of university policies and programs. For example, the Carnegie Commission on Higher Education recommends: "The approach to contract coverage should be one of restraint, with the contract covering economic benefits and with academic affairs left (or put) in the hands of the faculty senate or equivalent council" (1973, p. 49).

But I join those who believe that at most institutions where faculty bargaining takes place this separation cannot, in the long run, be maintained, for the machinery of the bargaining process will rise to encompass total faculty responsibility for, and involvement in, university governance.

Having said this, I must admit that thus far we have precious little data upon which to base such an observation. Indeed, we have precious little data about faculty bargaining. Most of the people who have written about faculty bargaining have exaggerated its incidence. In particular, as they offered numbers they often failed to stress that well over half the institutions engaging in bargaining are two-year colleges. At the risk of revealing an elitist bias, I call attention to the fact that no member of the prestigious Association of American Universities and no well-known four-year liberal arts college is yet bargaining with its faculty. This condition may quickly be corrected in the next academic year or two, but at present we are compelled to turn to community colleges and to emerging four-year state colleges and state universities for most of the available information about the process and progress of faculty bargaining.

Whatever the size and character of the institutional sample, it will always be difficult, although by no means impossible, to draw useful generalizations out of experience with faculty bargaining. This difficulty arises from the diversity and decentralization of the more than twenty-five hundred institutions that make up the American system of higher education. They range all the way from recently established community colleges to complex, multicampus multiversities, old and new, and encompass every level and type of public and private institution. This last difference is significant, for one of the striking curiosities or ironies of faculty collective bargaining is that at private colleges and universities the process is almost exclusively subject to federal law—to the National Labor Relations Act (NLRA) as interpreted and administered by the National Labor Relations Board (NLRB) and the federal courts.* Public institutions of all types, on the other hand, engage in faculty bargaining under state laws, interpreted and administered by state labor boards and state courts. Usually such bargaining is an aspect of public employee bargaining generally, for very few state statutes make any provision for faculty bargaining as a unique process requiring special attention. Although as many as thirty-nine or forty states are sometimes cited as having some measure of public employee bargaining, it is generally agreed that less than half the states have laws deemed applicable to faculties at public institutions. This condition, too, may change rapidly in the near future, for there are strong pressures on the legislatures of many of the inactive states to authorize public employee bargaining on a comprehensive basis. (In fact, state legislatures have been very active in this field in the past year or two, so a down-to-the-moment count of state laws is always elusive.)

There are many significant parallels between collective bargaining in private enterprise under federal law and the bargaining that takes place in the public sector under state law, for federal statutes and federal administrative and judicial rulings have substantially influenced state patterns. But faculties at public institutions in most states will nonetheless discover that their right to bargain dif-

---

*The NLRB has used its discretionary rule-making authority to limit its jurisdiction over private educational institutions to those having an annual gross revenue of at least $1 million for use in meeting operating expenses (35 Fed. Reg. 18370, December 3, 1970). It should also be noted that some fifteen states have passed "Little Wagner Acts" authorizing collective bargaining in certain types of private enterprise as a supplement to the bargaining authorized by federal law. Thus, faculty bargaining at an occasional private institution (St. John's University in New York City, for example) is taking place under a relevant state law rather than the federal statute.

fers in significant ways from that of their colleagues at private institutions. And vice versa.

who constitutes the "faculty"?

I now want to develop at considerably greater length a further and critically important observation: to describe the bargaining in which many educational institutions have thus far engaged as "faculty collective bargaining" is something less than wholly accurate. The conclusions that faculties at other institutions may draw from the examples presently available to them for study and possible action can be seriously misleading unless these faculties take a very careful look at what has been happening. I refer to the way the thorny and seemingly inescapable unit problem has been dealt with: who are the employees that may or must be recognized under the law as members of a single bargaining unit? The answer to that question—which may well be the most important question bearing on faculty collective bargaining—involves extremely complex legal, political and educational considerations.

The easy reference to "faculty bargaining," to which we are all prone, suggests that at most institutions something closely resembling the traditional faculty is bargaining as a unit with the governing board of the institution. But what is the traditional faculty? Do we mean those faculty members who hold the Ph.D. or equivalent degree or who are making significant progress toward such a degree?

Or do we include part-time faculty members—the adjunct teachers—whose professional preparation may well be substantially different and usually less demanding. And what about the so-called nonteaching professionals, registrars, physicians, and the like, who claim the status of professional but do little or no teaching or scholarly research? Are they part of the faculty, and if so, to what extent and in what numbers?

The American Association of University Professors once offered its solution to both of these issues of faculty inclusion or exclusion by restricting its "active members" to persons holding "at least a one-year appointment to a position of at least half-time teaching and/or research, with the rank of instructor or its equivalent or higher or other acceptable evidence, in an approved institution." But in 1972, the AAUP concluded that if it was to remain competitive with the American Federation of Teachers and the National Education Association as a bargaining agent candidate at many educational institutions, it must amend its constitution to admit to active membership, in addition to those who qualified under the older regulation, "any professional employee included in a collective representation unit with the faculty at an approved institution" (AAUP, 1971 and 1972).

"professionals" in the bargaining unit

Once the need arises to determine the membership of a bargaining unit in terms of an educational institution's employees who can, in one degree or another, claim a professional status and who perform an academic or educational function, we enter a thicket of confusion. There is, for example, a vast difference between the City University of New York and a private liberal arts college like Oberlin in the use made of part-time teaching personnel or in the number of nonteaching professionals needed to fulfill the institution's educational function.

It is difficult to know what figures to accept as accurate, but it appears that at CUNY some sixteen thousand professional employees were included in the single "instructional staff" bargaining unit at the beginning of the 1972-1973 academic year. The indications were that full-time classroom teachers, eligible for tenure, were a distinct minority within this group. The AAUP has estimated that at the State University of New York 30 percent of the members of the bargaining unit were ineligible for membership in the Association under its old rule prior to the 1972 change; that is, they were persons with a rank below that of instructor, or they were devoting less than half their time as university employees to teaching and research.

In opposing the aggressive commitment to collective bargaining adopted by the AAUP in 1972, the Association's president, first vice-president, and chairman of the Committee on Academic Freedom and Tenure stated that it should "be borne in mind that nonacademic professionals, who would probably be included in most appropriate bargaining units, amount to one-fourth to one-third of the total staff of some institutions." And they warned that, in accepting such employees into its membership as a result of the Association's role in faculty bargaining, it might well convert itself into an AAUP, "The American Union of University Professionals" (AAUP, 1972).

Thus far, all college or university employees included in "faculty" bargaining units have had to meet the test of being "professionals." But what is a profession? How does it differ from a trade, a vocation, or even a so-called semiprofession? (See Etzioni, 1969.) Law, medicine, and theology are sometimes referred to as "the ancient professions" and presumably that identification is more than enough to enable their present-day practitioners to call themselves professionals whenever that is to their advantage. Today, we usually concede the designation to persons in such further fields as engineering, accounting, architecture, and dentistry.

Is there "an academic profession"? Curiously, it is not recognized as one of the ancient professions, even though many lawyers, doctors, and theologians in the Middle Ages were often identified with universities and spent much of their time engaging in research or teaching their special knowledge to would-be practitioners in these three fields. It might thus be argued that the academic profession has always been "the master profession." Do today's college and university teachers primarily and customarily identify themselves as members of the academic profession? Or do they prefer to claim a professional identification with the disciplines in which they teach or engage in research, such as law, medicine, physics, chemistry, psychology, sociology, art, music, philosophy, or political science?

These questions pose interesting theoretical issues. Sociologists have produced a vast and varied literature in an attempt to develop a theory of professions (see, for example, Etzioni, 1969, and Parsons, 1968). But these questions also have practical consequences that cannot be avoided in faculty bargaining, either by the college professor who finds himself directly involved in collective bargaining or by the academic scholar who undertakes to observe and report on the bargaining process in academe. These questions cannot be avoided because the National Labor Relations Act and many state bargaining laws extend to "professional employees" the right, by majority vote, to detach themselves from an enterprise's nonprofessional employees, and then to bargain separately with management, or not to bargain at all. The NLRA defines "professional employee" in an exceedingly interesting fashion. The definition deserves to be quoted in its entirety:

The term "professional employee" means—(a) any employee engaged in work (i) predominantly intellectual and varied in character as opposed to routine mental, manual, mechanical, or physical work; (ii) involving the consistent exercise of discretion and judgment in its performance; (iii) of such a character that the output produced or the result accomplished cannot be standardized in relation to a given period of time; (iv) requiring knowledge of an advanced type in a field of science or learning customarily acquired by a prolonged course of specialized intellectual instruction and study in an institution of higher learning or a hospital, as distinguished from a general academic education or from an apprenticeship or from training in the performance of routine mental, manual, or physical processes [NLRA, 1935].

In spite of the seeming precision of the federal statute on this point, it is clear that the NLRB possesses and must exercise considerable discretion in deciding which employees of an educational institution do in fact meet all of the tests set forth in the statute. It is fair to conclude, I think, that up to now the NLRB has not gotten very far with the task of developing a useful common law on the issue. Shortly after the Board ruled in 1970 that private colleges and universities are compelled to bargain with their employees under federal law, the Board rejected a petition from the AAUP that it exercise its authority under the NLRA, as well as the federal Administrative Procedure Act, to hold hearings and accept testimony from a variety of spokesmen for higher education and then issue a series of rules that might guide everyone concerned in the determination of so-called representation or unit issues, as faculty bargaining in the private sector of higher education took shape.* The Board chose, instead, to develop such rules on a case-by-case basis. The rules that have thus far emerged are neither precise nor very helpful—certainly with respect to the issue of confining a bargaining unit to a university's professional employees. It does have to be conceded that the NLRB in most instances has made a much more responsible attempt to cope with this issue than have most state labor boards.

*The NLRB took jurisdiction over private higher education in a case involving certain nonacademic employees of Cornell University, therewith reversing a 1951 ruling in the Columbia University case (97 NLRB 424) in which it had refused to exercise its discretionary jurisdiction over private colleges and universities. See NLRB, 1970.

In voting to include part-time teachers and nonteaching professionals in faculty bargaining units, the NLRB has noted that these employees do appear to meet the statute's test of "professional employee." But the Board has offered very little documentation in support of these rulings. The evidence offered on this point at hearings, as well as the Board's own research into or understanding of the issue, have been very sketchy.

For example, in the early disputed representation case at the C. W. Post Center of Long Island University in 1971 (NLRB, 1971a), the Board, in accepting the AFT's position as the petitioner and rejecting the position of the university governing board, included twenty-seven librarians in the faculty unit, noting, among other things, that they all possessed master's degrees in library science. A chemistry laboratory assistant and a biology technical assistant were excluded on the finding that their work did not require them to possess advanced degrees in their fields. Guidance counselors were included on a finding that they "are required to have advance knowledge and are performing the intellectual and varied functions" contemplated by the words of the statute. The Board also found these counselors to be "qualified psychologists with psychology degrees." But the NLRB provided no further identification of the qualifications for the degrees. In including 206 part-time teachers in the unit, over the objection of the university governing board, the NLRB asserted that these employees "have the same educational background as their full-time faculty counterparts," but it offered no documentation of this rather unconvincing generalization.

Neither the NLRB nor any state labor board has yet shown an inclination to identify the Ph.D. or equivalent degree, or progress toward such a degree by an employee, as the proper test for including an employee in a faculty bargaining unit limited to "professionals." In fairness to the NLRB, however, it should be noted that apparently no such contention has ever been carefully made in a disputed representation case by any party to such a proceeding.

On the other hand, where there is no disagreement between the petitioning labor organization and the university governing board, the recognized bargaining unit may in fact be narrowly limited to the traditional faculty. Thus, in the recent NLRB ruling in the Syracuse University case (NLRB, 1973c), the AAUP, as the sole petitioner, and the "Employer" (to use the NLRB's word) were in agreement that the unit should be limited to "all full-time members of the faculty . . . excluding all other employees." The Syracuse faculty itself may recognize such nonteaching professionals as librarians or academic counselors as full-time members of its ranks, as have many faculties, but at least this would be a decision made by the academic community at Syracuse.

separate recognition of faculty members by discipline

How has the federal Board reacted to the possible argument that there is no such thing as an academic profession—that is, a general "faculty"—but only teachers and research scholars who are professionals in the sense of identification with particular disciplines? The Board has skirted the edges of this issue, but only in disputed cases where law or medical faculties have sought recognition as separate units or exclusion from a faculty bargaining unit entirely. In cases arising at Fordham and Catholic University—and more recently at New York University (NLRB, 1973b)—the NLRB voted to approve the wish of law faculties to be recognized as separate units (NLRB, 1971b and 1973a). In a case at Wayne State University, on the other hand, the Michigan Employment Relations Commission rejected the claim of the medical faculty for separate recognition (MERC, 1972). Up to now, so far as I know, no academic department at the undergraduate level has sought separate recognition.

That this issue of separate recognition of faculty members by disciplines is another thicket is perhaps beginning to be recognized by labor boards. Thus, in the recent Syracuse University case the NLRB members divided three to two in their response to the request of the Law Faculty Association that the law faculty be recognized as a separate unit. Both the AAUP and the University governing board sought a universitywide unit, except that the AAUP wanted department chairmen included and the governing board asked that fifty-three chairmen be excluded on the ground that they were "supervisors." The NLRB majority was not quite willing to adhere to the Fordham precedent, without qualification. Instead, it devised an elaborate voting procedure for the representation election by which the law faculty would vote separately on several questions. In effect, the Board's balloting instructions were intended to let the law faculty first decide whether or not it wished to be included in a universitywide faculty unit, and then, depending on how that vote turned out, whether it wanted to be represented by the AAUP, LFA, or neither. Because of the importance of the ruling and the bearing it may have on the way the NLRB henceforth applies the federal statute to private educational institutions, it will be helpful to examine a portion of the Board's opinion (NLRB, 1973b, pp. 9, 11):

> Relatively small in number, oriented more closely to their chosen field than to the academic or university world, with intellectual interests more nearly aligned with those of their brethren in practice than with their academic colleagues of the faculty, it is apparent that [the law faculty's] special interests may suffer if not recognized. The same is undoubtedly true of other disciplines, most particularly those requiring work at the graduate level to prepare for specialized areas of endeavor—as opposed to purely scholarly or intellectual pursuits. Such disciplines, more practical than intellectual, identifiable—we anticipate—by the relationship between their academic and practicing colleagues, are, at once, part of the academic world and foreign to it and to each other.

> ... it is the alignment of the law faculty with the distinctive traditions and interests of the legal profession that has influenced us strongly to give recognition to the law faculty's preferences as to whether they wish to remain separate, as lawyers, or to be conjoined with their fellows in their other profession—teaching.

Some of the rhetoric used in this NLRB opinion may seem to reveal a willingness to fashion a series of rules that would support the development of a special collective bargaining model for higher education, a model significantly different from that applied to private industry. Such a conclusion would be premature, however, for the issue in the Syracuse case was the narrow one of whether a law faculty is entitled to special treatment. The NLRB has shown a certain disposition to give law professors what they want; it has yet to reveal any comparable empathy with any other segment of the academic profession or any similar willingness to meet the requests for separate or special treatment by such segments.

department chairmen: labor or management?

I turn now to a brief look at a further troublesome issue in disputed unit determination cases that can result in failure to recognize a traditional faculty, as such, as the appropriate bargaining unit. This is the issue of whether department chairmen must be excluded from a faculty unit on the ground that they are supervisors as defined in the National Labor Relations Act and are thus part of a university's management rather than its labor force.

Proceeding on a case-by-case basis, the NLRB has ruled both ways on this issue. In the recent Syracuse case where, as we have seen, the AAUP asked that chairmen be included in the unit and the University governing board sought their exclusion, the NLRB ruled unanimously for exclusion. In the Board's defense, it must be noted that it has been making a valiant attempt to square the evidence presented by the parties in each disputed case with the statute's definition of a supervisor as an employee who either exercises direct authority, on behalf of management, over other employees—particularly with respect to hiring and firing—or whose recommendations to higher management persons have a high degree of "effectiveness."

One can sympathize with the NLRB's difficulties in determining how much authority department chairmen wield at each institution where the faculty has, through one or more labor organizations, sought a representation election; nevertheless, the Board's rulings to date have been quite confusing and the results chaotic. In the Syracuse case, the Board concluded that the evidence showed that chairmen did exercise authority as supervisors and must thus be excluded from the bargaining unit. Doubtless, chairmen do exercise more authority at Syracuse than they do at many other institutions, but the AAUP, as the petitioner in the case, nonetheless sought their inclusion, perhaps hoping that if faculty bargaining took shape at Syracuse a more suitable and limited role for chairmen could be negotiated at the bargaining table.

Be that as it may, any faculty that initiates action leading to a representation election, whether at a private or public institution, must recognize that if the status of chairmen becomes a disputed issue before a labor board, the decision may well go either way—in a ruling which, from a faculty's point of view, may reveal a confused and wholly unpredictable understanding of the function and authority of department chairmen. The chaotic character of the rulings thus far could have been avoided if federal and state labor boards had, except in some extreme situations present at certain authoritarian institutions, followed a general rule that chairmen are inevitably and inescapably part of a faculty and that if their status requires adjustment at an institution, such a result can be sought in the contract negotiations.

campus governance: senate-union competition

If faculty collective bargaining be viewed as a form, or at least as an aspect, of university governance, perhaps the most significant issue that will be settled as time goes by is whether faculty senates and faculty unions can continue to exist side by side, with an agreed upon division of authority and function in the governance system. Some observers are predicting the demise of faculty senates. They point out that labor relations statutes typically authorize negotiations on wages, hours, and conditions of employment, and that this language can and will encompass almost any issue of institutional policy in which the faculty is interested—the academic calendar, teaching loads and methods, faculty-student ratios, educational leave programs, retirement arrangements, and even tenure and academic freedom.

Although academe's experience with faculty bargaining is thus far so limited as to make conclusions difficult, it is still far from clear that faculty unions will supplant faculty senates as the principal agencies representing faculties in university governance. Indeed, at some institutions collective bargaining contracts create governance agencies of the senate type where none existed or where what existed was quite inadequate. The contract at Boston State College and the second contract at Southeastern Massachusetts University are significant examples.

What difference will it make if traditional faculty governance agencies, encompassed by the word "senate," are replaced by faculty "unions"? Again, it is too early to try to answer this question on the basis of experience. We can only speculate, using as a point of departure the contract provisions and the experience generally with bargaining in industry. These sources of information suggest that there may, indeed, be power changes ahead for everyone in the organization of a university where faculty bargaining takes shape. The changes are very likely to affect the functions and authority of trustees, administrators, and students, as well as the faculty. Let us ponder here only the possible impact of bargaining on the faculty.

Faculty senates are seldom fault-free. Some of these faults might well be absent from faculty unions. But a union is a union, and unions in industry have long revealed certain characteristics that most faculties would deem incompatible with their principles and goals. Labor unions are not famed for a tradition of strong internal democracy. Instead, they are often authoritarian organizations. In their politics they typically illustrate one-party rule and long-term control of office by a few powerful individuals. Self-aggrandizement and corruption have not been uncommon. Admittedly, faculties might change all this in the organization and operation of their unions. But unless a faculty can manage to bargain with its institution on a wholly voluntary and informal basis, an objective which will not in the long run prove easy to achieve, it must abide by the requirements of labor laws.

Where a faculty does undertake to democratize the "labor organization" through which it is bargaining, it is likely to find that, under law, it must adhere strictly to the one-man, one-vote rule in union organization and procedure. Why not? it may be asked. Would not this adherence be an appropriate triumph for egalitarianism among persons who have, as intellectuals, particularly insisted on the need for more complete equality of opportunity *and* achievement for all men and women in all social settings? Perhaps so. But there will be changes.

It is doubtful, for example, that the typical arrangements by which faculty senates, college committees, and other agencies give varying degrees of guaranteed representation to separate segments of a faculty (departments, divisions, schools, faculty ranks, and so on), without strict regard to the numbers of persons identified with these segments, can survive the one-man, one-vote requirement. As already noted, the presence of significant numbers of part-time teachers and nonteaching professionals in a faculty bargaining unit can profoundly alter traditional balances of power in the faculty's share of university policy making. Nontenured faculty members may gain increased authority all down the line in university affairs, where their numbers are large. But the indicated financial stringencies that most educational institutions will be facing for the forseeable future may well result in an increase in the number and thus the authority of senior faculty members in a faculty union, as fewer and fewer young persons are appointed to a faculty. Where the will is strong within a faculty to grant its junior members an unusual degree of opportunity to express new ideas, influence educational change, and be more generously rewarded, a senate might well be the preferred instrument for achieving such results.

potential threats to academic freedom and autonomy

Academic freedom—particularly that of the individual faculty member—may be in jeopardy under a collective bargaining system, for the majority may be readier to bargain away minority rights in a labor union setting than it would be in a faculty senate setting. Under traditional arrangements, faculties have more often than not been unusually generous in allowing their maverick members almost unlimited time and opportunity to argue their positions on disputed substantive issues before final votes are taken.

This solicitude for the nonconforming faculty member often extends up and down the line in encompassing, among other things, a general willingness to let the faculty member teach whatever courses he wishes to, or at least to teach prescribed courses in his own way. It can be argued that this emphasis on minority rights has become a fault at many institutions and is responsible, as much as any other single factor, for the faculty conservatism which, it is alleged, sabotages educational experimentation and change. But that a faculty union will be the center of educational ferment is doubtful!

Faculty bargaining is virtually certain to accentuate the process of external intrusion into policy making and administration at educational institutions, public and private, that is already well under way in this country. This intrusion will increasingly affect faculty interests and power. Labor boards will, as has already been seen, have the power to determine the membership of so-called faculty bargaining units; they will also exercise their power to declare certain institutional ways of doing things "unfair labor practices" and to order their discontinuation. This authority of labor boards extends to labor union practices as well as to those of management. Unfair labor practice rulings by labor boards are typically subject to judicial review. Federal and state courts may thus exercise new and final authority over matters that many academic communities have hitherto jealously guarded as among their own prerogatives. That few unfair labor practice rulings have yet been made against either management or labor in higher education does not mean that university managements and faculties will continue to be free of this kind of interference indefinitely.

An external intrusion that is already a reality under faculty bargaining is the power of a labor arbitrator, exercised at the final stage of the grievance processing system established by a collective bargaining contract, to alter solutions to disputed issues of faculty interest reached on campus. It is being argued that this authority of arbitrators can and should be restricted to correcting procedural mistakes and that an arbitrator's ruling should never replace that of a faculty agency on substantive academic issues or educational policies. But it is not yet clear that such a line between procedure and substance can be drawn effectively either in the terms of a contract or in the process of contract interpretation and administration.

separate bargaining laws for faculties?

The recent report of the Carnegie Commission on Higher Education (1973, p. 51) recognizes faculty bargaining as an appropriate governance model that will prove attractive to some faculties. Indeed, the Commission recommends that laws should be enacted in all fifty states giving faculties at public institutions full freedom to choose this model if they wish to do so. The Commission, however, wants the best of two worlds, for it prescribes a kind of faculty bargaining from which troublesome issues have been removed. For example, department chairmen would be included in bargaining units, and the terms of contract limited to economic benefits, with academic affairs left in the hands of a faculty senate or equivalent body.

Recognizing that these results may not prevail where labor boards exercise final authority to determine the membership of bargaining units and where statutes in effect render everything negotiable at the bargaining table, the Commission recommends that Congress and the state legislatures enact separate laws covering faculty members that would "be responsive to the special circumstances that surround their employment." If this is not done, the Commission recommends that separate provisions covering faculty bargaining should be included in comprehensive labor relations statutes, or that more "leeway" should be provided for special administrative rulings on faculty bargaining.

My own guess is that it will take a very much more favorable political attitude toward higher education in general—and toward faculties in particular—than now exists in Washington and virtually all state capitals before legislative bodies can or will be persuaded to find the time and willingness to authorize separate forms of collective bargaining for the academic profession. For the forseeable future, no faculty should adopt collective bargaining in the expectation that special laws will be enacted in time to enable them to avoid undesired consequences, such as the possibility that department chairmen may be excluded from faculty units. (The faculty member who is tempted to think that the exclusion of *his* chairman from the unit would not be an unmitigated disaster needs to remind himself that where chairmen are excluded from units it is because labor boards label them as supervisors and that this then provides governing boards, presidents, and deans with a strong basis for arguing that chairmen are indeed administrators and should be integrated into an institution's administrative hierarchy.)

summing up

One hesitates to draw any very sharp conclusions on the basis of faculty experience with collective bargaining through the 1973-1974 academic year. Where a "shared authority" model of university governance exists and is working reasonably well, I would counsel a faculty to proceed slowly toward replacing this model with one that incorporates collective bargaining into the governance system.

I recognize, however, that at some institutions collective bargaining has proved to be the means of bringing a governance system into being where none existed or where an existing system was quite unsatisfactory. Boston State College and Southeastern Massachusetts University provide examples. I also realize that collective bargaining has given the faculty a stronger voice in economic matters, where an existing governance system provided a satisfactory voice in academic matters, and that the two parallel systems have been "operational" without one threatening to supplant the other. Rutgers University perhaps exemplifies this result. But this latter arrangement must stand the test of time. I am troubled by the thought that a faculty union and a faculty senate will sooner or later be drawn into an inevitable power struggle and that the big guns and battalions will be found on the side of the union.

One recommendation of the Carnegie Commission I can endorse without any qualification whatsoever. That is that "faculties in each institution should undertake the most careful analysis of the implications of collective bargaining and, more broadly, of which of the alternative forms of governance they prefer" (1973, p. 48). I go a step beyond the Commission in reminding academics and particularly political scientists that they possess a special competence and thus a special responsibility to assist in these careful analyses. If we cannot help our institutions govern themselves more wisely and effectively, how can we presume to counsel our fellow citizens in the broader society in the continuing search for better political orders?

references

American Association of University Professors. "Association Membership." *AAUP Bulletin,* 1971, *57,* 324.

American Association of University Professors. "Council Position on Collective Bargaining." *AAUP Bulletin,* 1972, *58,* 46-61.

Carnegie Commission on Higher Education. *Governance of Higher Education: Six Priority Problems. A Report and Recommendations.* New York: McGraw-Hill, 1973.

Etzioni, A. (Ed.) *The Semi-Professions and Their Organizations: Teachers, Nurses, Social Workers.* New York: Free Press, 1969.

Michigan Employment Relations Commission. *Wayne State University,* R71B-58, R71B-75, R71B-79, and R71C-137, 1972.

National Labor Relations Act. § § 2 (12) and 9 (b) (1), 49 Stat. 449 (1935), as amended by Pub. L. No. 101 (1947) and Pub. L. No. 257 (1959); 29 U.S.C. § § 151-168 (1970).

National Labor Relations Board. Cornell University, 183 NLRB No. 41, 1970.

——— . C. W. Post Center, 189 NLRB No. 109, 1971a.

——— . Fordham University, 193 NLRB No. 23, 1971b.

——— . Catholic University, 201 NLRB No. 145, 1973a.

——— . New York University, 205 NLRB No. 16, 1973b.

——— . Syracuse University, 204 NLRB No. 85, 1973c.

Parsons, T. "Professions." In *International Encyclopedia of the Social Sciences.* Second Ed New York: Macmillan and Free Press, 1968.

Since 1970, Robert K. Carr has been the director of the Study Project on the Academic Profession of the American Council on Education, for which he and Daniel K. VanEyck prepared their 1973 book, Faculty Bargaining Comes to the Campus. *After twenty-six years as a faculty member and department chairman in government—first at the University of Oklahoma and then at Dartmouth College—he served for ten years as president of Oberlin College. Among his other activities, he served during 1957-1958 as general secretary of the American Association of University Professors.*

*A new phase of the faculty bargaining
movement has begun, with increased administrative
sophistication and student involvement; but only
enlightened policy makers can keep universities
from following the traditional industrial model.*

the search for
new models in
faculty bargaining

jack h. schuster

Collective bargaining among professionals in American education
dates back only to the early 1960s, with the success of the American Federation of Teachers (AFT/AFL-CIO) in organizing public
school teachers in several large cities. But already, at least in higher
education, we have moved from a phase dominated by union activism to an emerging phase of countervailing forces; and the forms
of faculty bargaining that develop from this second phase are unlikely to be simple extrapolations from the first.

phase one

In higher education, AFT locals were formed on many campuses in the labor-conscious New Deal era of the 1930s, but none
achieved recognition as a collective bargaining representative. Since
then, labor unions have lobbied vigorously for the enactment of

79

comprehensive state laws to permit public employees to bargain collectively. Their persistent efforts were rewarded first in Wisconsin in 1959 (although that statute's coverage did not extend to university faculty members) and then in Massachusetts and Michigan in 1965 and in New York in 1967. In none of these cases were university officials more than peripherally involved in the decision: in New York, for example, neither the governing boards nor administrations of the State University (SUNY) or the City University (CUNY) nor the State Department of Education took official positions on the enormously important Public Employees Fair Employment Act—the "Taylor Law."

Not long after exclusive bargaining agents were recognized for school district employees, faculty unionism began to emerge in higher education, initially at Dearborn, Michigan's Henry Ford Community College, then among specialized institutions such as Rhode Island's Bryant College of Business Administration in 1967 and the U.S. Merchant Marine Academy in 1968. But not until 1969, following enabling legislation, hotly contested recognition elections, and lengthy contract negotiations, did the first agreements take effect at universities: CUNY and Central Michigan.

Riding a swelling tide of public-sector collective bargaining, the process has spread rapidly. Indeed, since 1968, the number of campuses whose faculties are represented by exclusive bargaining agents has expanded sixfold, and the number of individuals covered by those bargaining contracts has increased by a factor of eight. As 1974 began, the magnitude of faculty collective bargaining was estimated to have grown to over 200 exclusive bargaining units representing college and university faculties. Approximately 70 percent of the bargaining units were located at two-year colleges, the remainder at four-year institutions (including multicampus systems). These units represent approximately eighty thousand university employees—of whom perhaps fifty-five thousand are full-time, ladder-rank, teaching faculty—on somewhat over 300 separate campuses.* Together the CUNY and SUNY behemoths account for approximately 16 percent of the institutions and 40 percent of the individuals currently covered by faculty contracts (see Ausseiker and Garbarino, 1973, and *Chronicle of Higher Education,* 1973, p. 9).

*The existence of multicampus systems such as CUNY (nineteen campuses) and SUNY (twenty-six campuses) largely accounts for the difference between the number of *bargaining units* and the larger number of *campuses* represented by bargaining units.

In June 1970 faculty bargaining at private institutions received a sizable boost when the National Labor Relations Board, acknowledging that it was entering into "a hitherto uncharted area," reversed a doctrine to which it had adhered for twenty years and, in the now famous Cornell University case, concluded that under appropriate circumstances it would assert jurisdiction over nonprofit, private educational institutions. Nevertheless, faculty unionism is still overwhelmingly a public-institution phenomenon.

During these early years, the advocates of collective bargaining maintained tactical superiority. The national offices and communications networks of the AFT and the National Education Association—and more recently the American Association of University Professors—functioned as important resources for state and local affiliates. Experienced professionals served on their national staffs; they maintained information clearinghouses on lobbying, representation election strategies, and negotiating tactics. Although the AFT and NEA were hampered by limited resources in the face of mounting requests from bargaining-prone faculty groups, theirs was the only game in town: no management-oriented counterpart existed for lobbying or negotiating activities. Only a very few administrators—such as Chancellor Albert H. Bowker, then at CUNY, and President William Boyd of Central Michigan University—had made their way through negotiations, and without any significant extramural help to draw on. The major higher education associations in Washington, such as the American Council on Education (ACE) and the National Association of State Universities and Land-Grant Colleges (NASULGC), had not yet delineated an appropriate role for themselves and were moving into the faculty bargaining thicket with the greatest caution.

phase two

The period of superior union tactical strength began to wane in 1971; Phase Two, characterized by more aggressive and better informed administrative action, had begun to take form. University officials initiated efforts to build better communication networks and "staff up." In 1973, several enterprises of potential value to university management were launched:

● In April of that year, an Academic Collective Bargaining Information Service was established jointly by the ACE, NASULGC, and the Association of American Colleges, thanks to a sizable grant from the Carnegie Corporation of New York; and a director was named in June.

• The College and University Personnel Association and the National Association of College and University Business Officers together launched a series of faculty collective bargaining seminars across the country to familiarize university administrators with the fundamentals of faculty collective bargaining; experienced negotiators from the management side of the bargaining table were prominent among the seminar leaders.

• During the summer of 1973, the Academy for Academic Personnel Administration was created "for the purpose of developing expertise regarding collective bargaining and related academic personnel matters," with a core membership of campus administrators who have acquired real-life bargaining-table experience.

• In addition, conferences on faculty bargaining have begun to proliferate, and an ambitious institute—the National Center for the Study of Collective Bargaining—has been established at Bernard Baruch College of the City University of New York. While accessible to faculty and administrators, these conferences and the Center are potentially helpful to experience-short, information-hungry administrators.

Phase Two is thus providing a catching-up opportunity, especially for administrators not yet operating with a faculty collective bargaining contract. More aggressive, knowledgeable administrative activity combined with lingering faculty caution may help explain the sharp decline in union election victories from 1972 through early 1974. (Another trend indicator is the number of first-time faculty collective bargaining that were signed. Data contracts at Baruch's Center show that while 32 contracts were adopted in 1971 and 60 in 1972, in 1973 only 16 had been signed through November 1.)

Nonetheless, the possibility of a massive, combined NEA-AFT union could conceivably alter the balance of power dramatically. Already at CUNY, the NEA-affiliated Legislative Conference and the United Federation of College Teachers (AFT) have merged to form one enormous bargaining unit, the Professional Staff Congress, representing sixteen thousand instructional staff members; the New York State Teachers Association (NEA) and the United Teachers of New York (AFT) have joined forces at the state level. At the national level, merger prospects fluctuate like the stock market. The NEA stipulated in July 1973 that its members must not be required to join the AFL-CIO, and this condition may well prove to be an insurmountable obstacle to merger; as of early 1974, merger talks have broken down. But, if the two organizations eventually are joined, they will have a combined membership of approximately 1.7 million, second in size in this nation only to the 2.2 million-member International Brotherhood of Teamsters. This development could profoundly affect the future development of collective bargaining. Currently, though, administrative advances have begun to offset initial union strength; and countervailing powers are much in evidence as the activities of both proponents and opponents of faculty bargaining are intensified.

As part of this second phase, three issues are emerging that deserve particular attention: the involvement of students as a countervailing power; the likely impact of new state legislation; and the consequences of collective bargaining for campus governance.

enter the student: a triangular bargaining table?

The role students are now beginning to play in the collective bargaining process deserves closer attention than it has yet received. Whether students will be able to secure a prominent position at the bargaining table is unclear. But early indications suggest that the future course of faculty bargaining will be influenced, perhaps significantly, by student efforts—with respect to both the shape of future legislation and the provisions of faculty union contracts.

The obstacles to broader student participation are formidable, for a dominant characteristic of collective bargaining is its bilateral nature. Two parties are involved, "employer" and "employee." Few concepts are embedded so deeply in American labor law. The advent of collective bargaining in the public sector complicates the scheme of things, because the identity of the public employer sometimes gets to be confusing. To determine what party has the ultimate authority to act on behalf of the "management" of a public agency may not be a simple task. When public monies are committed, executive agencies and legislative bodies are often drawn into the process. (For example, a state legislature may decline to appropriate sufficient funds to pay for the bargain struck by management with its employees. To complicate the issue further, the employee bargaining agent may well seek to lever the public employer through lobbying efforts directed at governors and legislators.) But even with the confusion arising from the blurred identity of the public employer, the principle of bilateralism—employer and employee—remains essentially intact.

Now enter the students. When first brought into contact with faculty unionism, student leaders instinctively were supportive. As Carr and VanEyck observe: "The initial reaction of students to faculty bargaining has been favorable. Faculty members voting to participate in collective bargaining are seen by students as at long last recognizing and asserting their valid interests and claims against a common enemy" (1973, p. 259). But the authors then suggest that student patience with faculty unionism may be short-lived:

> Students may yet discover that they get the short end of the stick when the administration and faculty play games together. . . . The naivete of the first student reactions to faculty bargaining will not persist if faculty bargaining patterns reveal to students that control of educational policy is shifting from the governance agencies on which they have representation to the bargaining agent substructure, where they have none [p. 259].

Because collective bargaining is fundamentally a political process, whether students are able to safeguard their interests vis-à-vis faculty and administrators ordinarily will depend primarily on their political muscle. (There are exceptions, such as the Massachusetts case discussed below.) The general rule raises the underlying question: what is the outlook for student clout during the formative years ahead?

Viewed in retrospect, the decade of the 1960s in American higher education belonged to the students. Student activism and "student power" rocked the education establishment. The concept of *in loco parentis* all but vanished. Research on students mushroomed. Curricula bent, if not yielded, to student pressures. At times, the nation's attention was riveted to this strange phenomenon. But with the winding down of the war in Southeast Asia, the curtailment of the draft, and a tighter labor market, the "student movement" all but faded from public view.

This quietude, however, obscures the fact that student leaders learned some important political lessons during the fitful sixties. Militant action was not the answer, though a case can surely be made that violent action and the implied threat of violence generated substantial concessions on college campuses. Student goals have shifted toward building a viable political counterforce. Aided immeasurably by the eighteen-year-old vote, this elusive objective has become a more realistic goal. The University of California Student Lobby, based in Sacramento, offers a prime example. Purporting to represent almost one hundred thousand UC students on nine campuses, the lobby has been very effective in defining and protecting student interests (Trombley, 1973). They have gotten concrete results—occasionally to the discomfort of the University's administration. Nor is California an isolated example (Semas, 1973b).

In Washington, D.C., the newly formed National Student Lobby has been carving out a place for itself amid the melange of education interest groups. Apparently the NSL exerted more influence during Congressional consideration of the complex student aid measures contained in both the Education Amendments of 1972 and the urgent Supplemental Appropriations Bill enacted in 1973 than did the National Student Association and other student groups in recent years (Trombley, 1972, and Humphrey, 1973). In all, students may be acquiring a level of sophistication and influence in Washington unprecedented for American students (Semas, 1973a). Such is indisputably the case in California. But how is the new political sophistication among student leaders likely to interact with the collective bargaining phenomenon?

Increasingly, students are coming to recognize how directly their interests are affected by faculty collective bargaining, and student involvement in the bargaining process has begun. In 1972, at the Brooklyn Center of Long Island University, students were conceded the opportunity to sit as observers at the bargaining table. At the University of Washington, the Graduate and Professional Student Senate had a bill introduced in the state legislature that would permit students to act as third parties during collective bargaining negotiations and to refer for arbitration binding on both union and administration those portions of the agreement relating to faculty working conditions.

But the most intriguing developments in student activity are occurring in three multicampus systems: two where collective bargaining experiences have been strikingly different—the City University of New York and the Massachusetts State College System—and one, the University of California, where faculty to date are not represented by an exclusive bargaining agent.

The University Student Senate at CUNY: Pitched Battle. By any standards, the long struggle over collective bargaining at CUNY has been intense and raucous (Mintz, 1971). The two contracts for separate faculty bargaining units, which took effect in September 1969, followed a fiercely contested election and prolonged negotiations. Both contracts expired August 31, 1972, but negotiations, mediation, and fact-finding over a renewed agreement were drawn out for almost a year and a settlement was not reached until July 1973.

Early on, the systemwide student government—the University Student Senate (USS)—recognized that the stakes for students were high and that collective bargaining was a powerful, even dominant, mechanism for shaping the education environment. Consequently, it has mounted an increasingly vigorous, hard-hitting campaign to defend what its officers perceived as student prerogatives. Led by Alan R. Shark (its chairman until early 1974), the USS has delineated student interests—including "teacher evaluations, required courses vs. electives, school calendars, master plans, fees and tuitions, penalties, probation, academic standing, space per student, holidays, library services, cafeteria services, etc." (Shark, n.d., p. 7). Identifying potential threats to those interests, the USS defended them against assaults resulting from the bargaining process. Even if bargaining was not tripartite, the USS left no doubt that *three* batteries of well-oiled mimeograph machines were spinning away throughout the long months of contract negotiation.

And the students managed to score some pretty good hits by regularly pounding away at targets of opportunity. "The paternalistic attitude that the [Board of Higher Education] and the union have some magical way of knowing what students' interests are, without asking students, has become as antiquated as Adam Smith's 'Invisible Hand,' " Shark wrote the *New York Times* (1972b). He sharply criticized the application of conventional collective bargaining models to higher education:

> While the industrial model has served industry well, institutions of higher learning were never intended to be factories. ... In the final analysis the burden of proof will lie on the shoulders of students, who must demonstrate that the present industrial model of collective bargaining is not suited to institutions of higher learning. The point must be stressed that one need not be an employee to enjoy the rights and protection that a negotiated contract provides [1973, pp. 9, 62].

And he proposed full-scale bargaining rights for students

> through "a collective bargaining unit of students." The terms
> and conditions of the contract would be collectively bar-
> gained for by a tripartite body of students, faculty, and ad-
> ministrators subject to the Board of Higher Education and
> the state legislature. Each campus would establish local chap-
> ters, with elected student leaders, which could utilize a modi-
> fied version of present student governments. These local orga-
> nizations would feed into a universitywide organization paral-
> leling the faculty structure when universitywide policies are
> affected. There would be one contract [Shark, 1972a, pp.
> 557-558].

As Frederic M. Brandes, the executive director of the USS, puts it
succinctly, "Since student interests are not represented at negotiations, it is student interests that must eventually suffer" (1973, p.
12).

The USS has picked its targets selectively, attempting, insofar
as possible, to preserve an independent posture. Thus it has expressed vigorous support for the union position on such crucial issues as limitations on class size and forcing the administration to
furnish reasons for the nonrenewal of a faculty member's contract.
But the brunt of the USS attack has been directed at the union.
"When faculty demand more money, more fringe benefits and reduced teaching loads," Shark asserts, "student tuition and fees may
rise or essential student services will be cut. Course offerings will be
reduced or programs phased out" (1973, p. 10). And Shark charged
that the first order of business of the merged union—the Professional Staff Congress—was to block student evaluations as illegal on the
grounds that only an evaluation system protecting staff rights and
negotiated by the PSC could be legal. "When it suits the PSC to
have student input they call on us," he claims, "but they're afraid
we'll speak out for student interests that may not agree with their
position. PSC keeps avoiding the real issue, 'How can you negotiate a contract which shapes, forms and directs students' education, without student input?' " (University Student Press Service,
n.d.).

Seeking to maintain its impetus and to establish further its
national leadership role, in 1973 the USS hosted the first national
student conference on collective bargaining. Now that CUNY's sec-

ond three-year contract has been signed, until negotiations begin on a third contract the USS will need to monitor the administration of the new contract and assert student interests within that context to maintain its current momentum; absent the high drama of negotiations on important and controversial issues, the USS may find this a difficult task. But all in all, the vigorous action of the USS may well be a precursor of how student governments in other institutions will react when drawn closer to the flame of collective bargaining.

Governance by Contract: Tripartite Bliss in Massachusetts. A few hundred miles away, but on the other side of the faculty collective bargaining globe, the Massachusetts State College System, consisting of nine state colleges, the Massachusetts College of Art, and the Massachusetts Maritime Academy, has adopted a radically different approach. Unlike most statewide systems, this one has no single bargaining agent representing the systemwide faculty. Rather, petitions and representation elections have been conducted on a campus-by-campus basis. On the several campuses where contracts are now in effect, the faculty have been represented in some instances by AFT locals, in others by NEA locals.

The Massachusetts situation is also remarkable in that, until a 1973 amendment, state law forbade collective negotiation on salaries and fringe benefits. The result has been contracts that cover virtually the entire apparatus for campus governance, including explicit provision for student participation, a labyrinthine structure of faculty committees, and election and recall of department chairmen.

The first contracts to be concluded—at Boston State and Worcester State—readily illustrate the extent to which the role of the union appears to have merged with functions ordinarily associated with faculty senates. For example, the twenty-nine-page Boston contract establishes an elaborate system of faculty committees at departmental, divisional, and campuswide levels. At the departmental level there are committees on faculty evaluation, on curriculum, and on faculty work load, scheduling, and course assignments. At the divisional level, each of the four divisions has a committee on reappointment, promotion, and tenure. At the campus level, there are committees on curriculum, on college development, and on budget consultation. In addition, an All-Campus Committee is expected "to coordinate the activities" of a committee on governance review and these other campuswide committees. This All-Campus Committee consists of nine faculty members (the president of the union as chairman plus eight other faculty members appointed by the union president and approved by the union's executive council), five students "determined by a campuswide election," and one administrator appointed by the president of the college "for the purpose of promoting good communication and understanding." (In the contract signed six months later for Worcester State, the comparable All-Campus Council consists of six students, six faculty, and six administrators.)

These contracts also provide in detail for student evaluation of teaching; the new student committees on faculty evaluation have mandates broad enough to strike terror into the heart of any student-evaluation-shy faculty. In these colleges, the pretty rhetoric extolling the virtues of student evaluation is bolstered by concrete contractual language.

Most administrators and trustees would shudder at the prospect of detailed "governance" matters penetrating the collective bargaining agreement, but such is not the case in Massachusetts. Donald E. Walters, the deputy director of the state college system, offers this rationale:

> If faculties are to prevent their reclassification as mere employees, if faculty professionalism and independence is to be preserved where it exists and sought after where it does not, if institutional autonomy is not to be eroded, and if college communities—faculty, students and administrators alike—are to emerge from the experience of unionization and collective bargaining as colleagues and not as adversaries, *then campus governance must become a matter of collective bargaining.* ... What is clearly being proposed, therefore, is that an approach to collective bargaining, in which *structure and governance are carefully introduced into a contract,* can act as a kind of restraint upon both parties, and minimize the scope of adversarial relationships to those matters for which there appears to be no alternative. By enlarging the role and responsibilities of faculty governance within the collective bargaining agreement, such alternatives are less necessary or sought after [1973a, emphasis added].

Massachusetts established an even more extraordinary precedent in 1973 when five student representatives were permitted to participate directly in the negotiation of the Fitchburg State College contract. The ground rules allowed the students to participate in all discussions, although they were not empowered to prevent the union and the board from reaching an agreement; after the contract was signed, the student body—as at Boston and Worcester—would conduct a referendum on contract provisions pertaining to student participation in decision making. According to Dr. Walters, the agreement "expresses the commitment on everybody's part to evolve the bargaining process into something that fits our institutions and doesn't just follow the industrial model" (*Chronicle of Higher Education,* 1973, pp. 1, 6; see also Walters, 1973b).

The Massachusetts contracts, viewed together, are unquestionably *sui generis.* But then, so is the environment from which those agreements have sprung: a public employment relations law that encourages collective negotiations but, until recently, precluded salaries from the scope of bargaining; faculties and students without deeply rooted traditions in shared authority; and, in Dr. Walters, an innovative administrator.

Harold L. Hodgkinson once observed that "the classic negotiations model is men on both sides of a table, one side representing management, the other representing labor. It is unlikely that any carpenter could make a table with enough sides to seat all the factions in a typical campus dispute" (1969). Now we are several years deeper into the faculty collective bargaining experience, and Hodgkinson's jest still rings true. But surely the Massachusetts model—a tripartite "negotiated system of campus governance" (Graham and Walters, 1973, p. 63)—comes closest to the imaginary table he envisions.

As striking as the Massachusetts developments are, they serve mostly to raise a host of questions about governance in general and student participation in particular. Are those Bay State students merely passive beneficiaries of fortuitous circumstances? Or do these unique contract provisions result at least in part from tough-minded student demands to be dealt a significant piece of the action? Most important, how have the contracts actually worked? Both the Boston and Worcester campuses by now have operated with their respective contracts for an academic year. Have the distinctions between the bargaining agent and faculty roles become as blurred in practice as they are merged in the language of the contract? Have students had a real impact—on faculty personnel decisions, on curriculum design, on budget priorities? Or has the ability of students to share in the shaping of campus directions been more illusory than real? Hopefully, answers to these questions will begin to surface in the months ahead.

University of California: The Student Lobby Enters the Fray. Students at Berkeley have won a well-deserved reputation for social activism. UC student leaders frequently have been instrumental in organizing lobbying efforts at local, state, and national levels. But despite a long history of student sympathy for various labor causes, the UC Student Lobby in Sacramento, maintained by the nine UC student governments, came down squarely in opposition to a conventional collective bargaining bill in its initial public stand on faculty unionism.

> To impose a rigid form of collective bargaining on higher education (particularly UC) would quickly freeze students out of all participation in areas of legitimate concern to them. The history of collective bargaining in higher education has shown that students are almost totally excluded from any participation once contracts begin to be negotiated between unions and management. . . .

> In higher education working conditions for faculty cannot be separated from questions of educational policy that directly affect students and are thus legitimate concerns of students. Examples of these issues include class size, number of course offerings, availability of professors for independent student projects, student evaluation of teaching in relation to the promotion process, and the whole area of curriculum planning and innovation. For years students have been working to become participants in the areas mentioned above. Their participation is essential if higher education is to effectively meet the needs of a changing society. Rigid collective bargaining threatens to exclude students from the process of decision making [University of California Student Lobby, 1973, pp. 1-2].

To sum up, the early days of student passivity or instinctive sympathy toward faculty unionism seem now to have vanished. The student role in collective bargaining is evolving in as many forms as there are localized environments. But some common threads, not readily apparent a year ago, are now becoming plainly visible. Students are beginning to understand more clearly the ways in which their interests may be jeopardized by faculty unionism. And unless collective bargaining somehow provides a vehicle for enhancing student participation, as may uniquely be the case in Massachusetts, students will be opposing faculty unionism with increasing vigor.

The triangular bargaining table has not yet been constructed, and perhaps it never will be. But at the moment, students appear to be making some progress in their bid to force faculty collective bargaining out of its fast-forming "industrial model" cast.

impact of state legislation: the california scene

Faculty collective bargaining thus far is overwhelmingly an Eastern and Midwest phenomenon. Instances of full-scale faculty unionism west of the Great Plains are scarce at the community college level and practically nonexistent among four-year institutions. That situation could change dramatically in the near future, for Oregon now has adopted a newly-amended comprehensive state law that permits faculties to organize, and the legislative pots are bubbling in California and Washington. The unfolding dramas in those two states—unlike the scenario several years ago in Michigan, Massachusetts, New York, and elsewhere—feature vigorous participation by all segments of the university community. And this many-sided debate affords at least the possibility, however slim, that new approaches to faculty bargaining may emerge in states that have not yet adopted enabling legislation.

The outcome of the debate in California, with its mammoth systems of higher education, is likely to have repercussions well beyond the boundaries of the Golden State. Compared to a growing number of states, California's movement toward collective bargaining in the public sector has been tentative and sporadic, resulting in not one but a series of three major public employment statutes. The first, enacted in 1961 and subsequently amended, covers all state employees, including, by interpretation, those of both the University of California and the nineteen-campus California State University and Colleges. As a "meet-and-confer" type statute, it gives employees the right "to form, join and participate in the activities of employee organizations of their own choosing for the purpose of representation on all matters of employer-employee relations," but provides neither for representation of employees by an exclusive bargaining agent nor for bilateral determination of employment issues. The second statute, which became law in 1965 largely as a result of pressure from the NEA-affiliated California Teachers Association to remove teachers from the more restrictive coverage of the first, requires school district employers (including the state's nearly one hundred public community colleges) "to meet and confer in good faith" with teachers. Negotiations must be conducted through a local "negotiating council" whose seats are allocated proportionately among qualified teacher organizations according to the size of their respective memberships. The third, enacted in 1968, applies to employees of cities, counties, and special districts; under its authority, "a number of cities and counties have enacted implementing ordinances and resolutions which vary considerably in their principal provisions."

Thus, as applied to California higher education, the statutory maze has the effect of providing one set of standards for employer-employee relations at four-year institutions and quite another for employees of community colleges. But this particular inconsistency is only one of the many considerations that have accelerated the movement toward legislative action to streamline existing laws.

Among the more salient political realities of labor relations in California are the state's approximately 1.1 million public employees (read "voters") and the growing strength and political action funds of public employee organizations. It should come as no surprise, therefore, that several influential state legislators, seeking higher state office, have been moved to champion collective bargaining legislation, seeking to capitalize on an important source of potential political support.

One measure which sought to establish full-scale collective bargaining for employees of school districts and postsecondary institutions was passed by the legislature in October 1973 but was promptly vetoed by Governor Ronald Reagan. It has been reintroduced. Also under consideration is the more ambitious statute proposed by the Assembly Advisory Council on Public Employee Relations. In its scholarly, innovative, and highly controversial report, this blue-ribbon panel recommends the repeal of the existing three statutes and enactment of perhaps the nation's most comprehensive version of public sector collective bargaining legislation, permitting collective bargaining throughout the public sector, creating a public employment relations board (PERB) with broad powers, and authorizing public employee strikes.* Addressing the issue of whether the proposed law should apply to academic personnel of the state's colleges and universities, the Advisory Council notes:

*Existing state laws give public employees the right to strike in Alaska, Hawaii, Pennsylvania, and Vermont. Other state statutes either forbid public sector strikes or are silent on the issue.

> There is nothing intrinsic in the teaching profession in institutions of higher learning that absolutely rules out collective bargaining as the alternative to present methods of faculty governance. Reasonable men can and do differ over the advisability of substituting collective bargaining for existing arrangements, and we express no opinion on that question. We do conclude, however, that the faculties of state colleges and universities should have the same rights and protections as other public employees in the state to decide for themselves whether they wish to organize in collective bargaining with their employers [California Assembly Advisory Council, 1973, p. 39].

The report has created no small degree of consternation within the higher education community. The Advisory Council appears to have relied quite heavily on testimony presented by faculty unions whose membership, at least at the University of California, consists of a small fraction of teaching faculty. But perhaps the most fundamental criticism has been the Advisory Council's approach to collective bargaining that makes all too few allowances for the distinctive characteristics of faculty-administration relations at a university where "shared authority" in governance has been a long-standing tradition.

Its strong statutory language on unit determination may well lead a PERB to conclude that teaching faculty and nonteaching professionals ought to be represented in a single unit; and its language concerning the scope of bargaining would seem to make eligible *all* governance issues for potential bilateral determination.

Meanwhile, other university-based proponents and opponents of faculty bargaining continue to slug it out. One notable combatant is the new Berkeley Faculty Association, a dues-paying membership organization of the UC Berkeley "ladder" faculty. Established by vote of the Berkeley faculty senate in 1972, its Senate-mandated responsibility is to "prepare for the eventuality of collective bargaining by continually informing itself and faculty on all relevant issues" and "monitor and attempt to influence any pending legislation that might be regarded as possibly authorizing collective bargaining on the part of public employees" (University of California Academic Senate, Berkeley Division, 1972, pp. ii-iv). This strategy, as envisioned by the Academic Senate, may come to serve as a model for other faculties who wish to protect their interests as a ladder faculty group vis-à-vis possible encroachments, through broad unit determinations, by part-time faculty and nonteaching professionals.

Regardless of the legislature's ultimate action on the proposed statute or rival measures, any public employment measure in California must be able to clear one major hurdle: the likelihood of a gubernatorial veto. Governor Reagan has made clear his irrevocable opposition to collective bargaining, arbitration, and the right to strike for public employees. "If someone chooses to work for the people, for the public instead of a profit-making enterprise," he has stated, "then he has to give up some things."

Given the Governor's position, proposals in California permitting full-scale collective bargaining for faculty probably will not become law prior to the 1974 elections for governor and legislature. After that, according to many observers, enactment may be merely a matter of time. But the form such legislation takes, and, just as important, the subsequent configuration of bargaining units, undoubtedly will have considerable influence on the development of public policy in states without comprehensive bargaining statutes. Unfortunately, though, there is little reason to believe that a bargaining model especially sensitive to the needs of the academy will emerge in California.

consequences for governance: the dominant issue

Despite collective bargaining's ostensible preoccupation with economic issues, the most important consequences for the life of the university revolve around bargaining's impact on governance. Most observers would concur with ACE President Roger W. Heyns about collective bargaining for faculty:

> Its effects on the academic profession and its potentials for strengthening or weakening the institutions and for helping or hindering teaching, research, and service are still not fully known. What is known is that the ramifications extend far beyond "wages, hours, and other terms and conditions of work" as they are understood in industrial bargaining [Carr and VanEyck, 1973, p. vii].

Unfortunately, a model for faculty collective bargaining patterned on the "industrial model" has already taken root, and universities, which are neither steel plants nor, for that matter, quite like any other public agency, are being forced into the industrial mold. The industrial model does not appear to be a comfortable fit; in fact, it may well be a calamitous fit. Other negotiating models tailored to the distinctive characteristics of the academy are urgently needed, at least to provide options. Yet few innovations thus far have appeared. With the possible exception of Massachusetts, it seems clear that neither "management" nor "labor" at four-year institutions has been very resourceful in designing faculty collective bargaining models. Over four years have elapsed since contracts were signed at Central Michigan and CUNY. In that period one might have hoped for some ingenuity in developing approaches to collective bargaining better contoured to the distinctive features of the academy. Instead, we have plunged ahead, not just borrowing but grafting great chunks from the "industrial bargaining model" embedded in the National Labor Relations Act.

Are other models really possible? Indeed, is the university *qua* employer distinctively different in any important sense—and, arguably, therefore deserving of special treatment? Many commentators have found persuasive the contentions of Sanford Kadish who, among others, has explicated eloquently the distinctive elements of the university, based largely upon the extraordinary, if not unique, role of its faculty manager-employees (1972). A growing number of persons, however, believes those considerations do not set the university apart and do not overshadow the faculty's status as employees.

Are there other nations from whom we might learn? At first glance, the answer would surely seem to be "no." After all, in no other country is the organization of higher education nearly so diverse and decentralized as it is in the United States. Accordingly, the bargaining models that have evolved in Great Britain, Canada, and elsewhere seem to offer little transferability to the American experience. Yet despite the obvious dissimilarities at the national level, there is still some reason for exploring the collective bargaining experience in other countries.

The system in Great Britain bears particular scrutiny. Since 1919, the Association of University Teachers (AUT) has represented the interests of the British professoriate. Though the AUT, strictly speaking, is not a trade union, it nonetheless does execute some trade union functions. A new negotiating machinery was developed in 1970 for determining salaries of university academic staff. It is a complex mechanism involving several rounds of negotiations between representatives of the AUT, the university, the University Grants Committee, and the government. Their unusual and intriguing model may have little relevance for the American experience, but it has enough tantalizing aspects that we in America ought to try to understand the model more clearly. (For more information, see Perkin, 1969, and Halsey and Trow, 1971.)

In Canada, developments moving toward faculty trade unionism have been quite recent, spurred on by the federal Public Service Staff Relations Act adopted by Parliament in 1967. While it is too early to tell much about how faculty bargaining will evolve in Canada, we should better familiarize ourselves with its characteristics (see Proulx, 1971, and Adell and Carter, 1972.) Experiences in other nations as well may be relevant. Glimpses into the procedures in both Sweden and Israel suggest that aggressive faculty bargaining can take place without spilling over into governance areas.

In summary, faculty collective bargaining is emerging as a catalyst destined to redistribute influence on campuses across the land. The most crucial issues, those revolving around institutional governance, have yet to be resolved. But unless new models for faculty bargaining are developed, the fragile academy may suffer irreparable harm in the years ahead.

references

Adell, B. L., and Carter, D. D. *Collective Bargaining for University Faculty in Canada.* Kingston, Ontario: Industrial Relations Center, Queen's University, 1972.

Agreement Between the Board of Trustees of State Colleges and the Boston State College Faculty Federation, American Federation of Teachers, Local 1943, AFL-CIO, April 3, 1972.

Aussieker, B., and Garbarino, J. W. "Measuring Faculty Unionism: Quantity and Quality." *Industrial Relations,* May 1973, *12,* pp. 117-124.

Brandes, F. M. "Point of View." *Chronicle of Higher Education,* April 16, 1973.

California Assembly Advisory Council on Public Employee Relations. "Report and Proposed Statute." Sacramento: Assembly Office of Research, State Capitol, March 15, 1973.

Carr, R. K., and VanEyck, D. K. *Collective Bargaining Comes to the Campus.* Washington: American Council on Education, 1973.

Chronicle of Higher Education, January 15, 1973.

Graham, D. L., and Walters, D. E. "Bargaining Process." In E. D. Duryea, R. S. Fisk, and Associates. *Faculty Unions and Collective Bargaining.* San Francisco: Jossey-Bass, 1973.

Halsey, A. H., and Trow, M. *The British Academics.* Cambridge, Mass.: Harvard University Press, 1971.

Hodgkinson, H. L. "The Next Decade of Campus Governance." Paper pre
sented at the Higher Education Executive Associates Conference, Philadelphia, November 6-8, 1969.

Humphrey, H. *Congressional Record,* March 6, 1973, p. S.3958.

Kadish, S. H. "The Theory of the Profession and Its Predicament." *AAUP Bulletin,* Summer 1972, *58,* 120-125.

Ladd, E. C., and Lipset, S. M., "Unionizing the Professoriate," *Change,* Summer 1973, *5,* 38-44.

McHugh, W. "Collective Bargaining and the College Student," *Journal of Higher Education,* 1971, *42,* 175-185.

Mintz, B., "The CUNY Experience." *Wisconsin Law Review,* 1971, No. 1,
112-120.

Perkin, H., *Key Profession: The History of the Association of University
Teachers.* London: Routledge & Kegan Paul, 1969.

Proulx, P. -P. "Collective Negotiations in Higher Education—Canada," *Wisconsin Law Review,* 1971, No. 1, 178-186.

Semas, P. W. *Chronicle of Higher Education,* April 30, 1973b, p. 4.

Semas, P. W. *Chronicle of Higher Education,* March 12, 1973a, p. 5.

Shark, A. R. "The Students' Right to Collective Bargaining." Unpublished paper, n.d.

Shark, A. R. "A Student's Collective Thought on Bargaining." *Journal of Higher Education,* 1972a, *43,* 552-558.

Shark, A. R. Letter to the Editor. *New York Times,* December 16, 1972b,

Shark, A. R. "A Student's Right to Collective Bargaining," *Change,* 1973, *5,*
pp. 9, 10, 62.

Trombley, W., *Los Angeles Times,* May 18, 1973.

Trombley, W., *Los Angeles Times,* April 28, 1972, pp. 1, 25.

University of California Student Lobby. "Testimony on SB 400," August 14,
1973. Sacramento: The Lobby, 1973.

University Student Press Service (CUNY). "Students Barred from Faculty Negotiations." News release, n.d.

Walters, D. E. "Comment." *College Management,* 1973a, *8,* 6-7.

Walters, D. E. "Collective Bargaining: Helping to Restore Collegiality." *The
Chronicle of Higher Education,* November 26, 1973b, p. 24.

*Jack H. Schuster wears three hats at the University
of California, Berkeley: assistant to the
chancellor; project director, faculty unionism
study, Center for Research and Development in
Higher Education; and lecturer in political science.
A graduate of Tulane University, he earned a
master's degree in political science at Columbia
and his law degree at the Harvard Law School.
From 1967 to 1970 he served as legislative
assistant and then administrative assistant to
Congressman John Brademas of Indiana.*

Sources of additional information and
expert assistance on faculty
unionism and collective bargaining.

for further information

jack h. schuster

Although the literature on faculty unionism has ballooned in the past several years, only fragmentary evidence is presently available on the post-contract, institutional experience with faculty collective bargaining. Unfortunately, research to date has ignored almost totally the *impact* of collective bargaining, especially on institutional governance at four-year institutions. Instead, the literature has been dominated by such preliminary (albeit indispensable) topics as labor relations in the public sector; survey research on faculty attitudes toward faculty unionism; the many-faceted legal aspects of faculty unionism, including criteria for unit determination and scope of bargaining; the dynamics of and strategies utilized at various stages of bargaining; and typologies of bargaining models. The focus on these preliminaries is understandable insofar as faculty unionism is new and few institutions have as yet accumulated as much as a year's experience under a contract.

Fortunately the situation is changing, and the time is ripe for students of higher education to examine some of the consequences of faculty unionism for campus governance. The superb study by Robert K. Carr and Daniel K. VanEyck, *Collective Bargaining Comes to the Campus* (American Council on Education, 1973), is the most helpful general book published thus far; and E. D. Duryea, Robert S. Fisk, and associates have assembled a series of useful articles in *Faculty Unions and Collective Bargaining* (Jossey-Bass, 1973).

In addition, Everett C. Ladd and Seymour Martin Lipset's report for the Carnegie Commission on Higher Education, *Professors, Unions and American Higher Education* (McGraw-Hill, 1973), presents a helpful overview. Also notable is a special section on collective bargaining published in the November 26, 1973, issue of the *Chronicle of Higher Education.*

Finally, the reader will find useful two sizable volumes edited by Terrence N. Tice: *Faculty Power: Collective Bargaining on Campus* (Institute of Continuing Legal Education, Ann Arbor, 1972) and, especially, *Faculty Bargaining in the Seventies* (Institute of Continuing Legal Education, Ann Arbor, 1973).

The most comprehensive recent bibliography on faculty unionism is available for $3 from the National Center for the Study of Collective Bargaining in Higher Education, Baruch College, The City University of New York, 17 Lexington Avenue, New York, New York 10010. Titled *Collective Bargaining in Higher Education, 1971-73* and compiled by John C. Allen, it includes references to arbitration awards, unit and NLRB decisions, and previous bibliographies. An earlier, shorter bibliography, *Collective Bargaining on Campus* (American Association for Higher Education, 1972), was compiled and annotated by Carol H. Shulman and published as the second in the ERIC-AAHE series of reports (AAHE members, $1.50; others, $2).

Among the several national sources of information identified in the previous chapter, these three are of particular value:

The Academic Collective Bargaining Information Service, directed by Dennis H. Blumer, distributes short papers and provides the names of consultants. Address: 1818 R Street, N.W., Washington, D.C. 20036. Telephone: (202)387-3760.

The members of the Academy for Academic Personnel Administration have acquired much bargaining table experience. For membership information, contact the AAPA president, Neil S. Bucklew, Vice Provost, Central Michigan University, Mount Pleasant, Michigan 48858. Telephone: (517)774-3151.

The National Center for the Study of Collective Bargaining in Higher Education at Bernard Baruch College, City University of New York, 17 Lexington Avenue, New York, New York 10010, under the direction of Maurice C. Benowitz, is undertaking research, publishing a newsletter, conducting conferences, compiling special bibliographies on request, and maintaining a computer-assisted system for retrieving information about clauses in bargaining contracts. Telephone: (212)725-3390.

index